QuickClicks

REFERENCE

MICROSOFT®

ACCESS 2010

CAREERTRACK.

QuickClicks Access 2010 Reference Guide

Trademarks

Disclaimer

The QuickClicks Reference Guide series is dedicated to all of CareerTrack's devoted customers. Our customers' commitment to continuing education and professional development inspired the creation of the award-winning *Unlocking the Secrets* CD-ROM series and the *QuickClicks Reference Guide* series.

Thank you for your continued support!

Contents

contents

Design

Automate

Collaborate

Appendices

Introduction

Congratulations on your purchase of *QuickClicks: Microsoft Access 2010*. You have invested wisely in yourself and taken a step forward with regard to your personal and professional development.

This reference guide is an important tool in your productivity toolbox, allowing you to maximize your productivity by effectively using the database functions within Microsoft Access. The tips in this reference guide are written for users who have a basic understanding of databases and at least one year of experience using other Microsoft Office applications.

Anatomy of a Tip

Each tip displays the tip title in the top left corner and the tip category on the top right, so you always know where you are and what you are learning. Each tip is written in plain English to help you find what you are looking for. Where appropriate, the tips include "What Microsoft Calls It" references so you can learn the lingo and perform more effective searches for additional feature capabilities in Microsoft's help system.

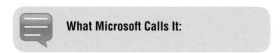

What Microsoft Calls It:

Each tip is assigned a difficulty value from one to four, with one circle representing the easiest tips and four circles representing the hardest.

Difficulty: ●○○○

All tips begin with an explanation, including a description of the feature and how the feature might be used in a business setting. A set of easy-to-follow instructions follows with lettered callouts that point to important parts of the screen. The displayed names of all selections and buttons are bolded and easy to find.

Extras Include the Following:

Icon	Name	What It Means
	Bright Idea	Bright Ideas provide additional information about Access or the features in question.
	Hot Tip	Hot Tips share functions and features, or additional uses of the features and functions, related to the one being demonstrated.
	Caution	Cautions draw attention to situations where you might find yourself tripped up by a particularly complicated operation, instances when making an incorrect choice will cause you more work to correct, or times when very similar options might be confusing.

There are two other bonuses that do not have miniature icons. They are displayed at the end of tips, where appropriate. These are:

Icon	Name	What It Means
	Options	Options represent places where there are two or more ways to accomplish a task or where two or more results might be obtained depending on the choices you make. Option icons appear within the text and all relevant choices are next to the icon.
	Quickest Click	Quickest Clicks indicate there is a faster way to accomplish the same task taught in the tip. Shortcuts like this, though, may leave out important steps that help you understand the feature. Therefore, each tip teaches the most complete method for accomplishing a task, and a Microsoft Quickest Click appears if there is a faster option.

At the bottom of each page, you will see either a Continue or a Stop icon. These icons indicate if the tip continues on the next page or if it is complete.

Understanding Access

Microsoft Access is a very powerful, useful application. When used correctly and efficiently, it can help you maximize your data storage, analysis, and output. It can do all of this—and save you a lot of time. However, to create a database with this tool, it is essential that you understand the type of database you are creating, and that you put time and thought into how you want your data collected, stored, and used before you start building.

For example, you might create an Access database to store customer information, keep track of product inventory, or catalog a collection of antique coins. Perhaps you work for a large organization and you need to keep employee information on file. In any of these cases, you may have a large amount of data in several categories that all relate to one another by one or more pieces of information— like customer number, date, and attribute.

"Relates" is the key word that introduces what is behind an Access database. Access databases are considered "relational." This type of database places information in multiple tables and then connects or links them together for viewing or analysis. This works best with information that is used over and over again. The information is spread out into tables so that it only has to be entered and maintained in one place. This makes it easier to enter, to update, and to avoid mistakes. For example, if you are an independent consultant and you want to track your clients, projects, expenses, and invoices, you might create separate tables for each group of data. Your client table might include information such as Client Name, Address, Phone Number, and Customer Number. Your project table might include information such as Project Name, Project Length, Project Description, Start Date, and End Date. These two tables "relate" to one another by Customer (most likely using a customer number or ID as a common field in each table). By creating separate tables for this information, you can maintain smaller chunks of information, connecting them when you want to see them combined, but not have to enter every piece of information into every table. In other words, you don't have to input your customer's phone number in each table. If you want your customer's phone number to display in results with your invoice information, you can create a query and/or report to pull this information from each table.

While Microsoft Access has certain features and functions that are similar to Word or Excel, it is a database built to be a multi-user program. That means that multiple people can work in the database at one time. As an Access administrator, you can build in security/permissions to protect or open usage for all or part of your database.

Getting Started with Access

Database Design

Now that you have purchased and installed Access 2010, you are probably eager to build your database, load your data, and begin using this powerful desktop database tool. A well-designed database can serve you accurate and up-to-date information in the format you need it. A poorly-designed database, however, can cause frustration, errors, and more work than you had without it. Since you will spend a great deal of time entering your data into your database, it makes sense to spend a little time beforehand making sure your database is going to meet your needs.

Determine How Your Database Will be Used

Though it seems obvious, thinking through all the tasks you expect your database to perform is key to making sure your design is going to meet your needs. You do not want to get to the end of the process and realize that you need to see how long it has been since a donor contributed to your charity, only to realize that you have no fields that record the dates of their past donations, for example!

Take the time to write a mission statement that you can refer to throughout the design process to remind you of the requirements your database must meet.

Identify Required Information

Knowing what data you will need to store is the first step in creating a database that will work for you or your business. If you do not have a place to store a piece of information, you will not be able to call upon it later! Start by studying any existing information that you already store in some way. This might include items you fill out on a purchase order or customer information that you store in an Excel spreadsheet or file cabinet. If you plan to use your database for financial records, look at bank statements, bills, and budget reports as a source for potential data fields.

Next, think through the types of reports, financial analysis, and mailings you might want to produce from the database. Imagine the information that would be required to generate those reports and form letters and make sure it is on your list. You might even consider drafting sample reports to get a sense of what blanks your database is going to fill in. Remember to think creatively. What questions might you want the database to answer once it is complete that you can't answer now?

Finally, spend time digging into the details of your information. For example, you know you need to store first and last names of your charity's donors, but have you also included a field that stores a proper salutation for each person? Ms. Touchydonor may be offended if your form letter addresses her with a generic "Dear Mrs. Touchydonor." Similarly, if you plan to collect e-mail addresses for sales leads, do you also need to store a record of whether the lead subscribes to your mailing list or has opted out?

Planning Your Tables

To make your database as efficient, for you, as possible, start by sorting your information into broad categories. A product sales database might organize their data around the categories of Customers, Products, Suppliers and Orders. A charity might organize their data into Donors, Volunteers, Donations, and Recipients.

Don't be tempted to combine information into one table. It might seem reasonable, for example, for Customer data to be gathered in your orders database. But if your customer makes many orders over time (and you hope they will!), you'll have to re-enter their information every time. By creating separate Customer and Orders tables, you can easily reference the customer with a single field. If the customer information changes, you only have to change it in one place.

Three good rules to keep in mind:

1. Break your information down into its smallest useful parts.

2. Always try to store each fact (or piece of information) just one time. If you find yourself typing in the same information in more than one place, pull it out into its own table.

3. Each table should only store related information. Don't create fields that belong in other categories. In our example above, you would not store customer addresses in your Orders table. That information is about the customer, so that information should live in the Customer table. Not only does this keep information organized, you won't have to change the information in two places if the customer's address changes.

Plan Your Fields

Now that you know what tables you're going to need, you can begin planning the fields within each table. Begin by referring to the lists of information that you identified as necessary and sketch a first set of fields. For your donor database, you might have decided that you need to collect: Name, Address, E-mail address, and Birthday (because you send a special honor card on each donor's birthday).

Then, look at your list and refine further. You will most likely want to create separate fields for First Name and Last Name so you can sort and index on just those columns later. It is also customary to split an address into it basic components: Address, City, State, Zip, and Country/Region. This can provide you lots of information later by allowing you to find all your donors who live in the same state, for example, or sending a targeted letter only to those donors who live in the same city as an event.

Finally, don't include calculated data in your Table. For the most part, you will not want to perform calculations in your table. That information comes from queries and reports.

See Also: Create a New Table

Identify your Primary Keys

Each table you create will contain a field or set of fields that uniquely identifies each record. This can be an ID number, such as an employee's social security number, a serial number for a product, or an ID number of your own design that is unique for each record. You may assign a Donor ID to each of the giving units in your Donor database, for example.

Important facts for creating your primary keys:

1. Values in the primary key field must always be different for each record. Names, for example, are not good as a primary key because you may have two John Smiths in your company. If you already have values, such as a product number for each item you sell, then you can use that information as your primary key. If you do not have such unique identifiers for your table, Access can create a field and assign record IDs for you.

2. A primary key must always have a value. Do not use a field that is sometimes empty as a primary key.

3. Choose a field whose value will not change. Once your database is built and many queries, reports and other tables are relying on your table, you do not want to have to change the name of your primary key in all those places. Don't use Department Name as your primary key, for example. Businesses are sometimes reorganized and department names change. You don't want to have to track down every place you need to change when "Marketing" becomes "Sales & Marketing." Use the department's ID code that will not change, even if the name does.

See Also: Assign a Primary Key

Create Relationships

Access is a relational database. This means that your information is divided into separate, category-grouped tables. Relationships between the tables then share the information in the specific ways needed.

One-To-Many Relationship

This is where planning our tables pays off. A One-To-Many relationship represents those times you found yourself typing the same information into the record over and over. For example, in your Orders table, you decided to create a separate Customer table so that you wouldn't have to type in the customer's information every time they made a new order. You create "One" record and use it "Many" times. This is the most common type of relationship in most databases.

In your Orders' table, you will include a field for "Customer ID" and create a relationship to the Customer table. The "one" side of the relationship *must* be a Primary Key.

Test Your Database

Once you feel like your database is ready to receive your information, take the time to give it a test drive. Populate your tables with sample data and work with the information for a while before you commit a lot of time entering your data. Create some queries and some reports; enter a few new records to help highlight potential problems. Make sure your database is going to answer the questions you want it to answer. Refer to your mission statement and confirm that the database is achieving its goals. Here are some questions to ask as you kick the tires on your new tool:

Did you forget anything? Make sure that all the information you are going to need is accounted for. If something is missing, identify where that piece of information needs to go. You may need to create a new field in a table, or you may need to create a new table.

Is anything extra or redundant? Look for fields that are unnecessary because they can be derived from other fields and remove the ones you don't need. You may realize that you don't need a field in your Donors database for "average giving level" because you can calculate that information in the donations table.

Are you entering the same information over and over? If you find yourself repeating information, you should consider dividing your information into more tables that have a one-to-many relationship.

Do you have tables with empty fields and few records? You may need to redesign so that tables are not so narrowly focused as to contain too few records. If you have many empty fields in each record, you may want to remove the ones that are frequently blank.

Is each record broken down into the smallest units?

Does each field match the table's category?

Are all the relationships that you will need between tables represented by common fields?

Congratulations!

You may find that perfecting your database is an ongoing process. You may create new tables and fields as your data evolves over time. You will also discover that it is much harder to make major changes once your data is imported and you have users, depending on the database. To plan your database before you begin using it is time well spent.

Getting Around Access

Items Seen in the Access Window

Microsoft Access works similarly to most other Microsoft 2010 applications in terms of window structure and basic functions.

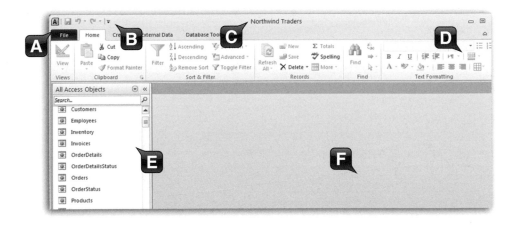

The Access Window

A File Tab	Click this button to access the Windows Menu to locate Open, Save, Print, Publish, Properties, and other Access options.	
B Quick Acces Toolbar	Place items here for quick and easy access. The Save button is a default tool in the Quick Access Toolbar. Click this button when you need to save your database or database object.	
C Title Bar	View the title and file type of the active database.	
D Ribbon/Groups	Locate Access menu items and controls.	
E Navigation Bar/ Pane	Display database objects of the type you select.	
F Object Window	Display any open database object.	

Database Objects

Tables, Forms, Queries, and Reports are the basic objects used in a database. There are a multitude of controls, functions, specifications, and parameters used in and for these objects. It is important to understand each object and its purpose within your database so you can select where to enter, retrieve, analyze, and output your data in the most efficient manner.

Tables: All data is stored in tables. The columns are referred to as fields, and rows are referred to as records. Each field contains the same type of data, such as a name or number. Each record is a set of fields relating to a specific entry. For example, you might create a table that contains all the contact information for the employees who work for you. A field might contain the employee's name. The complete record for each employee might include name, phone number, address, start date with the organization, and other basic information.

Forms: Forms are objects that make it easier to view or enter data in a table (or query). Since tables present information in an unrefined design mode, sometimes this information is hard to view or awkward to enter. A form displays the data in neatly arranged fields, with descriptive text to indicate what the contents should be. For example, there are 800 employees listed in your employee table. Each record includes 10 different pieces of information. Looking at this table in Access is not easy on the eyes. A form shows one record at a time, which is much easier to view and update. Simple forms can be created with a few clicks and save tremendous time and effort entering data into a table.

Queries: Queries are objects that enable Access to quickly find records that meet the specifications you request. For example, in your Employee Table, you want to find the employees with a last name starting with the letter B whose hire date was in 2004. To search through hundreds of records manually in your table might take hours. A query can ask specifically for that information from your table and

Access will find it—reporting only that data you asked for—within seconds.

Reports: Reports allow you to display data in an easy-to-read manner, in the layout and structure that you define. For example, you have a query set up to pull all employees whose hire date falls within the last quarter of the previous year. The finance department needs this list for their quarterly finance meeting, as these employees are eligible for a small merit increase. Instead of providing them with a raw list of employees,

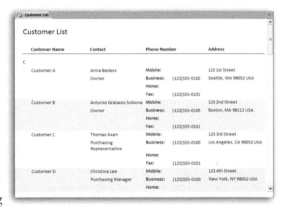

the Report tools within Access creates a polished report, presents the information in the format you want, and sends it to your colleagues.

Access 2010 File Formats

Access 2007 and later use new file formats available to replace the older .mdb files, as well as some additional options which include:

.accdb – The default file name extension for databases in Access 2010.

.accdc – The file name extension for Access 2010, known as an **Access Deployment** file. An **Access Deployment** file includes an application file and a digital signature. This file format assures users that no one changes the application file after you have created, saved, and/or published it. You can apply this format to any **.accdb** or **.accde** files.

.accde – The file name extension for Access 2010 files that are compiled into an "execute only" file. This prevents users from accessing the design elements of the application.

.accdr – This is the file name extension for Access 2010 files that enable you to open a database in runtime mode. When you change a database's file extension from .accdb to .accdr, you create a "locked-down" version of your database. Change the file extension back to **.accdb** to restore full functionality.

.accdt – The file name extension for Access 2010 database templates.

Backstage View

In Access 2010, Microsoft Office introduced the **Backstage** view. The **Backstage** view is where you will manage your databases and the information about them —creating, saving, security options, and customized settings. It is where you will find everything you want to do to a file that you don't do in the file.

Click the **File** tab **A** to access the **Backstage** view.

- The **Info** **B** tab will be selected by default. From the **Info** tab you can control access to your database from the **Encrypt with Password** button **C** and run the **Compact & Repair** tool **D**. The **View and edit database properties** link **E** opens the **Properties** dialog box where you can edit author and keyword information and view database statistics.

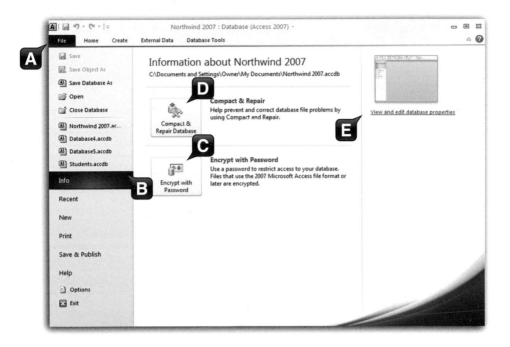

- Your most common tasks such as **Save**, **Save As**, **Open**, and **Close** are located at the top of the **File** menu 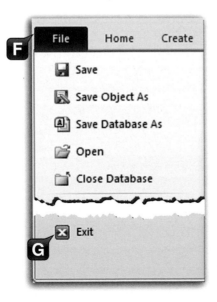. **Exit** is located at the bottom **G**.

- The **Recent**  tab opens a pane that displays the most **Recent Databases**
  you have opened.

Use the **Recent** tab to open files you access frequently without having to browse through many folders to find them.

If you open many databases every day, you can **Pin** your most important files to the top of the list. Click any grey pin **J** on the **Recent Databases** list. The pin will turn blue **K** and the file will jump to the top of the list where it will remain until you unpin it. Click the blue pin to unpin the item.

- The **New** tab **L** is where you will open a new workbook by choosing from Excel's many built-in **Available Templates M**. More templates are available under the **Office.com Templates N** heading (internet connection required). A preview of each template will appear in the **Preview Pane O**. Click the **Create** button **P** to open the template you've chosen.

- The **Print Q** tab offers some common print options. Send the active object to the printer by clicking **Quick Print** button **R** (prints directly) or the **Print** button **S** (opens the **Print** dialog box). Check the **Print Preview** button **T** frequently to open the **Print Preview** tab where you can see how your object will be printed as you are working with it.

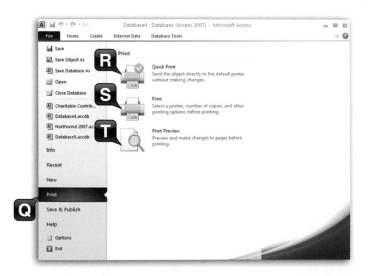

- The **Save & Publish** tab  is where you will find tools to save your database in the correct file formats and publish it to Access Services or SharePoint.

- The **Help** tab is where you can go to find answers to questions and problems you may be having.

- The **Options** tab launches the **Excel Options** dialog box.

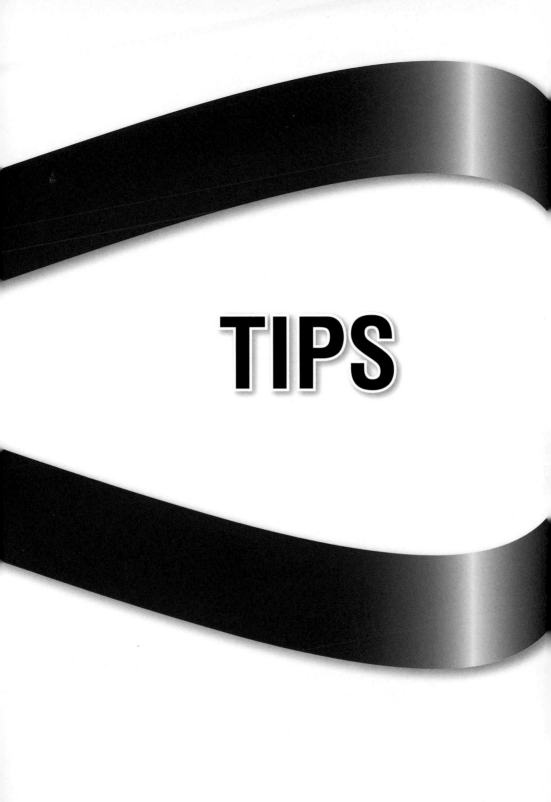

TIPS

1 | Create a New Table

Difficulty: ●○○○

PROBLEM You have information on products, customers, and distributors for a new small business. You are creating a database for your new small business. You want to create a database to enter and use your data.

SOLUTION Create Tables to store your data. Tables are the foundation of a database, containing all the data necessary to work with. Tables should store data about only one type of object. For a new business, one table should be created for each of the objects. In this instance, the Products table might include Product ID, Product Name, Product Release Date, and similar information; the Customers table might include Customer ID, Customer Name, Address, and other contact information; and the Distributors table might include Wholesale Price, Manufacturer Information, and Product ID.

See Also: Assign a Primary Key

Step-by-Step

1. Click the **Create** tab **A**.
2. Click **Table Design B** in the **Tables** group.

3. In the **Field Properties** pane, type a name for the first field in the first row of the **Field Name** column **C**. Press the **Tab** key on the keyboard to move to the next field.

4. In the **Data Type** column **D**, click the dropdown and select a data type. This should be selected based on the type of data entered into this field. If the data is a monetary amount, select **Currency**. Other options include **Text**, **Date/Time**, etc. Press the **Tab** key on the keyboard to move to the next field.

5. In the **Description** column **E**, enter text that describes what this field is asking for. This field is optional but can be useful as a reminder for what data the field requires. *Note: Repeat steps 3–7 to enter multiple fields into your table.*

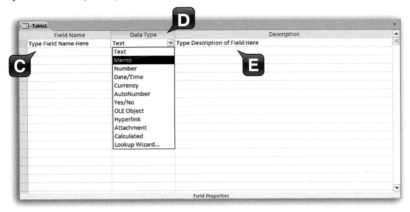

6. Click the **Save** 💾 button or type **CTRL+S** to save your table.

7. Every table should be given a **Primary Key**, or a value that makes each record unique from all other records in the table. This **Primary Key** might be the Customer ID or Product ID, for example. When prompted to set a primary key, click one of the following:

   Yes – Access will assign a primary key.

   No – Access will create the table without a primary key.

   Cancel – Continue without saving your table.

Entering Data into a Table

There are many methods for entering data into a table. Data can be manually entered in the **DataSheet View**, imported from another source (like an Excel spreadsheet), or through a form.

2 | Assign a Primary Key

Difficulty: ●○○○

PROBLEM You are creating a new database for the small charity you run. You have just completed creating a Donors table and you want your donors' addresses and personal information to be available to your other tables and queries so you don't have to repeat that information in other records.

SOLUTION Assign a Primary Key. Each table should have one field that is unique for each record in that table. This helps Access distinguish one record from another and link tables. Examples might be social security numbers in an employee database, an invoice number in a billing system, or e-mail address in a website membership database. This field is called a Primary Key.

- It is a field index that is unique for every record in that table—no duplicates.
- Primary keys *must* be used if you will be using relationships between tables.
- There will only be one primary key per table, although you can use multiple fields as the key.

See Also: Getting Started with Access—Database Design, Create a New Table

Step-by-Step

Assign a Primary Key:

1. Open the table in the object window.

2. If not already, switch your view to **Design** view by clicking the **Design View** menu option 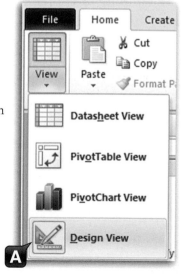 in the **View** dropdown menu in the **Views** group on the **Home** tab.

3. Click the field that you want to be your **Primary Key**.

4. Click the **Design** tab **B** under the **Table Tools** contextual tab.

5. Click the **Primary Key** button **C** in the **Design** group. An icon of a key will appear by the field that you have set as **Primary Key D**.

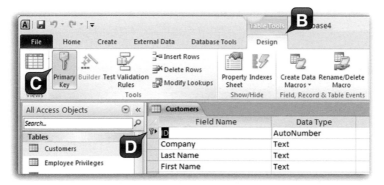

 **Step-by-Step**

Use AutoNumber to Populate your Primary Key

If your data doesn't have any fields that would make a good primary key (such as a product name or social security number), you can either choose an arbitrary, unique number system of your own design or you can use the **AutoNumber** data type in Access.

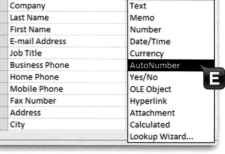

1. Create a field in your table that identifies the **Primary Key**, *exp: Donor ID, Department Code.*

2. In **Design** view, click on the dropdown arrow in the **Data Type** column of **Primary Key** field.

3. Select **AutoNumber E**.

STOP

3 Create a Field for Pictures, Files, or Hyperlinks

Difficulty: ●○○○

PROBLEM You want to store photos of your employees from their ID badges with their personal information in a table, so that anyone with database access can pull up an image of an employee at a glance.

SOLUTION Access 2010 allows you to attach files or images (.bmp, .pdf, .doc, etc.) to a record.

Step-by-Step

1. Open the table you want to work with in the object window.

2. If not already, switch your view into **Design** by clicking the **Design View** menu option in the **View** dropdown menu in the **Views** group.

3. Add a new field to your table **A**.

4. Click the dropdown to set the data type to **Attachment** **B**.

5. Click the **Save** button or type **CTRL+S** to save your table.

6. View your table in **Datasheet View** and note that your **Attachments** field contains a paper clip in the cells .

7. To add an attachment to a record, double-click the cell. Access supports the following graphic file formats without plug-ins:

.bmp Windows Bitmap
.rle Run Length Encoded Bitmap
.dib Device Independent Bitmap
.gif Graphics Interchange Format
.jpeg/.jpg Joint Photographic Experts Group
.exif Exchangeable File Format
.png Portable Network Graphics
.tif/.tiff Tagged Image File Format
.ico/.icon Icon
.wmf Windows Metafile
.emf Enhanced Metafile

In addition, you can attach many kind of files such as .log Log files, .text/.txt files and .zip files, for example. Some files types that pose security risks are blocked, but in general, any file that was created by Office 2007-2010 can be attached to a record.

8. In the **Attachments** dialog box, click the **Add** button **D**.

CONTINUE

9. In the **Choose File** dialog box, browse to the graphic you want to select, then click the **Open** button.

10. You should see the image's file name  **E** in the **Attachments** dialog box.

11. Click the **OK** button.

12. The cell that you added the file to should now have a number **1** next to it, indicating that you have an attachment included **F**.

Hot Tip: If you have multiple files or file types to add to a single cell, this function allows you to add multiple files to a single cell. For example, perhaps you have two photo images of employees—one photo from their identification badge and another from the employee directory. To add multiple files, follow the instructions above after adding the first file. The number will change to display the number of files you've attached to the cell.

ID Badge Picture
📎(2)
📎(0)
📎(0)
📎(0)

Bright Idea: To open/view your attachment(s), double-click the cell to open the **Attachments** dialog box. Highlight the file name and select **Open** or **Save As** to work with the file.

Caution: Once the data type is set to **Attachment**, it cannot be changed to another data type. You can, however, delete the field. All the attachments will get deleted as well.

Hot Tip: Certain types of files (such as image files) may be large in size and take up a lot of space. Consider the file size and how many attachments you will want to use. You may try using hyperlinks to connect to files that are in another location on a shared network. Access 2010 compresses some file types (bitmaps, Windows Metafiles, .exif, Icons, and .Tif/Tiff) as they are added.

STOP

4 | Create a Lookup Field

Difficulty: ●○○○

PROBLEM You have a table called "Departments" with fields for Department Name and Department Code (e.g., finance cost code or abbreviation). You have another table called "Employee List" that includes Employee Name, Contact Information, and Department (including Department Code).

When entering Department Code into your Employee List table, you would like an easier way to enter the information than looking up and retyping it from the other table.

SOLUTION Use a Lookup Field. A lookup field will pull the Department Name field options from the Departments table and provide a list of available options to save time and avoid data-entry errors.

One benefit of using a relational database, instead of a fat spreadsheet, is that while each object created may have a small number of defined fields, you can compare and link objects to create complex analyses.

 **Step-by-Step**

Create a Lookup Field

1. Open the table you want to work with in the object window.

2. If not already, switch your view into **Design** by clicking the **Design View** menu option in the **View** dropdown menu in the **Views** group.

3. Click the **Data Type** cell **A** for the field you want to define as a **Lookup Field**.

4. In the **Tools** group in the **Design** tab, click the **Modify Lookups** button **B** to open the **Lookup Wizard** dialog box. Or, in the cell, click the dropdown and select **Lookup Wizard** **C**.

5. To pull the field data from another table or query, click the **I want the lookup field to look up the values in a table or query** radio button  and click the **Next** button.

6. Select the table or query where you want to search for the selected values  and click the **Next** button.

7. Click the field(s) from which you want to pull the values and add them to the **Selected Fields** box 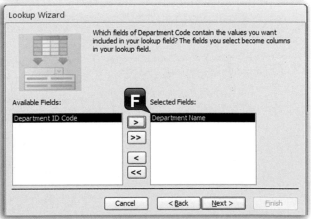 using the [>] button.

8. Click the **Next** button.

9. Sort the values in the field by **Ascending** or **Descending** order. Repeat the sort selection for each field you selected.

   a. Click the dropdown in the textbox to select a **Field** name .

   b. Click the button marked **Ascending**  to reveal **Ascending** order or click it again to toggle to **Descending**.

10. Click the **Next** button.

11. Adjust the width of the column and the display of your lookup fields. Place your cursor on the edge of the column until you get a double arrow , and click and drag the column to your desired width (or double-click to Autofit).

12. Click the **Next** button.

13. Type in a name for your **Lookup** field .

> **Options:** If you allow multiple values in a field, check the **Allow Multiple Values** checkbox . You might use multiple values if, for example, the data field you look at is called "Certifications" and the data allows for multiple certifications listed in the field.

14. Click the **Finish** button . If prompted to save the table before relationships can be created, click the **OK** button.

15. Switch to **Datasheet View** and check your work. You should see a dropdown menu appear when you click on a cell in the **Lookup** field.

STOP

5 | Create Forms Quickly with AutoForm

Difficulty: ●○○○

PROBLEM Your company has launched a lead generating initiative, and hundreds of new customers need to be added to your database quickly. You have a table that stores your customers' information, but creating a complex form takes a great deal of time and effort to produce. You need a fast and easy solution.

SOLUTION Create a quick, simple form to gather information in Access in just a few clicks.

Step-by-Step

---

1. In the **Navigation Pane**, click once on the table you want to use to create your form **A**. You do not need to open the table in your database window.

2. Click the **Create** tab **B**.

3. In the **Forms** group, click the **Form** button **C**.

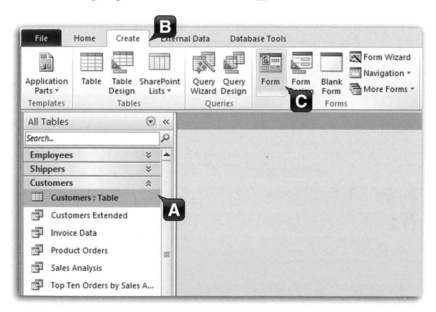

Access will generate a single item form 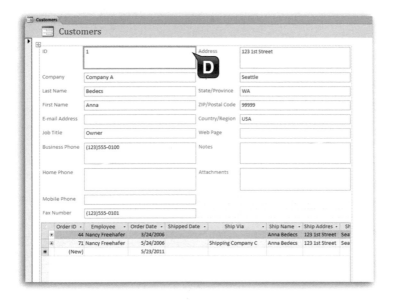 based on the fields included in the Table. A single item form displays information about one record at a time. All fields from the underlying data source are added to the form. Your form is ready to use immediately, or you can modify it in **Layout** view or **Design** view.

4. Save your form by clicking the **Save** button or pressing **CTRL+S**.

5. Click the dropdown **View** button in the **Views** group on the **Home** tab and select **Form View** 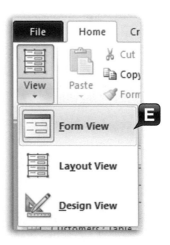.

6. Begin using your form.

6 | Create a Form with the Wizard

Difficulty: ●○○○

PROBLEM Most of the data used in your database was imported or entered by one person. Many different people will enter information into the database, now that the original data is in place. A simple form does not meet your needs. For the sake of consistency and ease of use, you want a form that includes all the needed data fields in the right order, and it must look polished and professional. You need to create a more intricate form.

SOLUTION Use the Form Wizard as an easy way to get started. Decide which fields to include, where to place the fields, and the order in which the fields are to be arranged or tabbed. The Form Wizard helps with the form foundation in a few quick and easy steps.

Step-by-Step

Use the Form Wizard

1. Click the **Create** tab **A**.

2. Click the **Form Wizard B** button in the **Forms** group.

3. Click the **Tables/Queries** dropdown **C** to choose the table that provides the fields for your form.

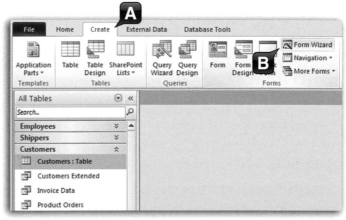

4. Select field(s) in the **Available Fields** box **D**, then:
   - Click ⊃ to add a single field at a time to the **Selected Fields** box **E** or
   - Click ⊃⊃ to add all fields.

5. If you want to include fields from multiple tables and queries in your form, choose another table or query from the **Tables/Queries** dropdown and add more fields to the **Selected Fields** box.

6. When all the fields from all the **Tables** and **Queries** you want have been added, click the **Next** button.

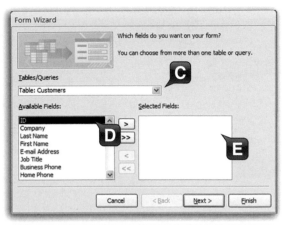

7. Select the layout for the form **F**. As you click on each of the radio buttons for the layout, Access shows you what each layout looks like.

8. Click the **Next** button.

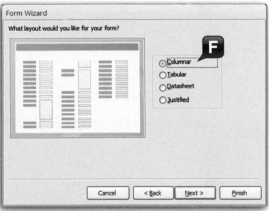

9. Type a name/title for your form **G**. Since others may use this form, the name/title should be clear to users.

10. Select one of the radio buttons to **Open the form to view or enter information** or to **Modify the form's design**.

11. Click the **Finish** button.

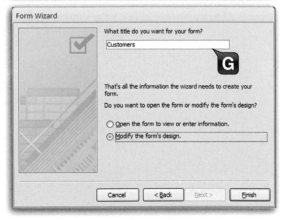

7 Create a New Query

Difficulty: ●○○○

PROBLEM In your Student Database, you have Guardian information in a table. You want to create an Emergency Contact List. You only want to pull the contact name and contact information (such as phone numbers and e-mail addresses), without including the rest of the information you have in the database for each Guardian.

SOLUTION Use the Query Wizard. The Query Wizard asks Access to search through records from a table or another query to find specific information. Access only grabs the data asked for. Pull exactly the data you want—and leave out the data you don't need.

Step-by-Step

1. Click the **Create** tab **A** and click the **Query Wizard** button **B** in the **Queries** group to open the **New Query** dialog box.

2. Select **Simple Query Wizard** and click the **OK** button.

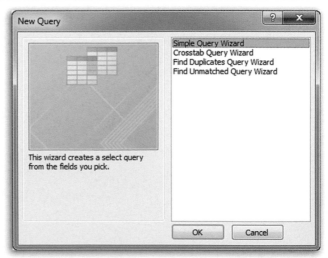

3. Select the table or other query from which you will pull data **C**.

4. Select the fields the new query will use by moving the field names from the **Available Fields** box **D** into the **Selected Fields** box **E** using the add **F** or add-all button **G**.

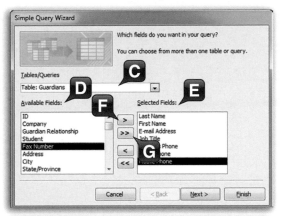

5. Click the **Next** button.

6. Select the **Detail** radio button **H** under the **Would you like a detail or summary query?** question. 🌢

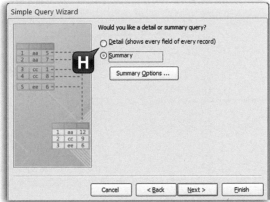

7. Click the **Next** button.

8. Enter a title for the query in the **What title do you want for your query?** textbox 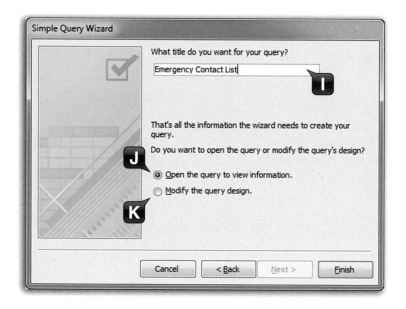 and select whether you want to open and view the query results **J** in datasheet view, or modify the query **K** further in design view.

9. Click the **Finish** button to close the wizard.

Simple Query Wizard

What title do you want for your query?

Emergency Contact List

That's all the information the wizard needs to create your query.

Do you want to open the query or modify the query's design?

◉ Open the query to view information.
○ Modify the query design.

Cancel   < Back   Next >   Finish

Hot Tip: To quickly create a query that performs some basic functions, click the **Summary** radio button 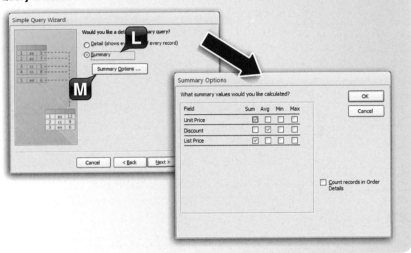 **L**, then click the **Summary Options** button **M** under the **Would you like a detail or summary query?** dialog box question. This will open the **Summary Options** dialog box where you can choose **Sum**, **Average**, **Min**, or **Max** calculations per field. Make your selections, then click **OK** to return to the **Simple Query Wizard**.

8 Create a New Relationship

Difficulty: ●●●○

PROBLEM You have finished all the new tables for the private high school that you run. All your Primary Keys have been assigned and all the shared fields have been created in the tables that need to share data. You need a way to tell Access to link your tables together to complete your relational database.

SOLUTION Create a new table relationship. If you want to search or report on data across tables, they should be related. Tables can only be related if there is a matching field in both of them.

- Relationships should not be set up until all tables have been created and tested.
- Relationships in Access are most often "One-To-Many" relationships, i.e. a single record in one table can be related to many records in another table. (Example: One student can have up to nine teachers each year.)
- The "one" side of the relationship must be a Primary Key.

 Step-by-Step

Create a New Relationship

1. Open the database and then click on the **Database Tools** tab **A**.

2. Click the **Relationships** button **B** to open the **Relationships** window **C**.

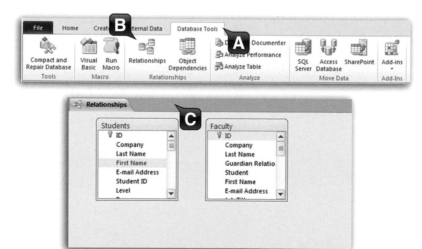

3. If the tables you wish to link are not already displayed in the **Relationships** window, click the **Show Table**  button in the **Relationships** group on the **Design** tab to open the **Show Table** dialog box. 🌢 ✳

4. Select the table that needs to be linked and then click the **Add** button. Repeat until all the tables you want to relate are available in the **Relationships** window. Click **Close** when you are finished.

5. To link your tables, double-click in the background of the **Relationships** window to launch the **Edit Relationships** dialog box.

6. Click the **Create New** 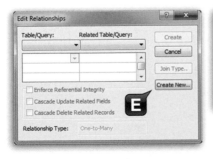 button to launch the **Create New** dialog box.

7. In the **Left Table Name** dropdown **F**, select the table you want to relate. In the **Left Column Name** dropdown **G**, select the table's **Primary Key** field.

8. In the **Right Table Name** dropdown **H**, select the table you want to relate it to. In the **Right Column Name** dropdown **I**, select the field in the second table that is the same data as the field you chose in the first table. The selected field does not have to be the primary key.

CONTINUE

Create a New Relationship   **23**

9. Click **OK** to return to the **Edit Relationships** dialog box. You will see the linked fields in the dialog box.

10. To specify advanced relationships, click the **Join Type** button 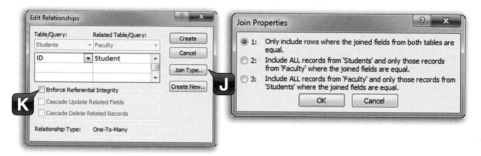 to open the **Join Properties** dialog box. Select the type of **Join** you want to create:

- **Option 1 = Inner Join:** Only include rows where the joined fields from both tables are equal.

- **Option 2 = Left Outer Join:** Include ALL records from 'Students' and only those records from 'Faculty' where the joined fields are equal.

- **Option 3 = Right Outer Join:** Include ALL records from 'Faculty' and only those records from 'Students' where the joined fields are equal.

Click **OK** to return to the **Edit Relationships** dialog box.

11. If you want Access to notify you if you add or delete a record in one table that would affect the integrity of a linked table, click the **Enforce Referential Integrity** checkbox **K** and choose your cascade options.

12. Repeat **Create New** as needed or click **Create** or **OK** to apply the relationships. Lines will appear in the **Relationship** view that show your new links **L**. If you have chosen a **Left outer** or **Right outer join**, an arrow will be shown on the relationship line **M**. This arrow points to the side of the relationship that shows only matching rows.

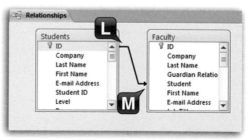

Step-by-Step

Edit an Existing Relationship

1. In the **Relationships** window, right-click on any line connecting two tables and select **Edit** to open the **Edit Relationships** dialog box **M**.

2. Make your changes in the dialog box, then click **OK** to apply your changes.

Quickest Click: Right-click in the background of the **Relationships** window and select **Show table** to open the dialog box. Double-click in the background to open the **Edit Relationships** dialog box.

Hot Tip: You can also create relationships between queries and tables. To add links between queries or between queries and tables, click on the **Queries** tab to view available queries or the **Both** tab **N** in the **Show Table** dialog to show both queries and tables.

Bright Idea: Editing the relationships is a great way to "fix" an existing database that is poorly designed without losing your original data.

9 Create and Run Report

Difficulty: ●●○○

PROBLEM One of your customers wants to see all of the products they purchased in the last year. You would like to present the information in a way that you can e-mail to the client for easy viewing and printing.

SOLUTION Run a Report. Reports present information from the database in an easy-to-read format, and they are designed for better printing than query results. There are three ways to run a report. You can view it, print it, or e-mail it. The type of output you create for your report depends upon how it will be used.

Step-by-Step

Create Report

1. Click on the **Create** tab **A**.

2. Click on the **Report Design** button **B** in the **Reports** group to open a blank report in **Design** view in the object window.

3. The **Report Design Tools** contextual tab **C** will appear. Click the **Design** tab. If the **Field List** task pane **D** does not automatically display on the right side of the screen, click on the **Add Existing Fields** button **E** in the **Tools** group.

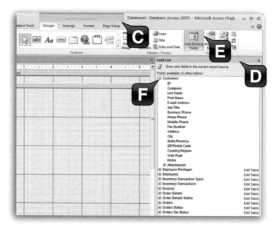

4. Click the **Expand** button **F** of any table in the **Field List** to see the available fields for that table.

5. Select and drag fields from the **Field List** task pane to the **Detail** section of the report **G**. You can click and drag field boxes on to organize the report items out exactly the way you want. 💡

6. Add images, logos, titles, page numbers, controls, or date and time information to your report by using more report design tools in the **Header/Footer H** and **Controls** group **I**.

7. After you have selected all the fields you want included in your report and completed your design, click **Save** or **CTRL+S** to open the **Save As** dialog box. Type a name for the report, then click the **OK** button.

Step-by-Step

Report Output

To **Run** and choose how your report is distributed, choose one of the following:

View Report:

1. Click the **Report View** dropdown option **J** in the **Views** group on the **Home** tab to see the report data in the object window. ❋

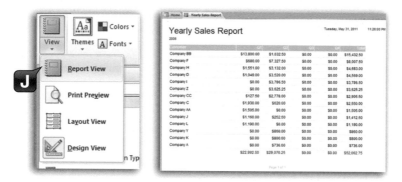

Print Report:

1. Click the **Print Preview** dropdown option **K** in the **Views** group on the **Home** tab to open the **Print Preview** tab **L** and see a print view of the report in the object window.

2. Set print options in the **Page Size** and **Page Layout** groups.

3. Click the **Print** button **M** to send the report to the printer or click **Close Print Preview** **N** to return to your last view.

E-mail Report:

1. Click the **Print Preview** dropdown option **K** in the **Views** group on the **Home** tab to open the **Print Preview** tab **L** and see a print view of the report in the object window.

2. In the **Data** group, click the **E-mail** button **O** to open the **Send Object As** dialog box.

3. Choose the format you want your report exported to from the **Select output format:** box **P**.

4. Click **OK** to export the report and open an e-mail message with the report as an attachment **Q**. *Note: Microsoft Outlook must be set as your default e-mail client to use this feature.*

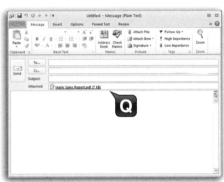

Caution: When important or confidential information is e-mailed, you may want to select a file type that does not allow the reader to manipulate the data.

Bright Idea: Use **AutoReport** to convert an entire query into a report.

Quickest Click: Click the **Report View** button in the bottom right corner of the application window.

Hot Tip: If you don't use Outlook as your default e-mail client, or you want to save a report to your computer to send as an attachment at some other time, click on one of the other options in the **Data** group **R** on the **Print Preview** tab.

STOP

10 Create a Grouped Report

Difficulty: ●●○○

PROBLEM You want to know which of your products are most profitable. You have a query that shows you all your orders for the past quarter, but you don't want to add up the individual product totals manually.

SOLUTION Create a grouped report. Microsoft Access 2010 allows you to create a basic grouped report using the Report Wizard, or you can add grouping and sorting to an existing report.

See Also: Create and Run Report

Step-by-Step

1. Open the query or table you want to modify in the object window.

2. Click the **Create** tab, then click the **Report** button **A** in the **Reports** group.

3. Access will generate a quick, tabular report in the object window and activate the **Report Layout Tools** contextual tab **B**. Edit the report layout in **Layout View** until it fits to one page width before applying any grouping or sorting. To delete any unwanted columns from the form, right-click on the column title, then select **Delete Column C**.

4. Right-click the column you want to group or sort, then click **Group On (field name)** 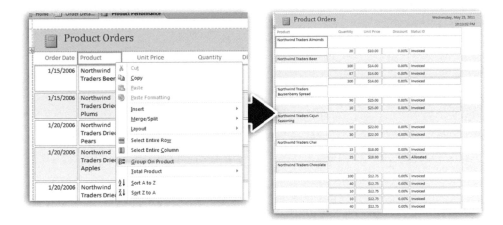. Access will move the grouping field to the leftmost column, and group the rest of the columns based on that column. Access may also add a grand total to the **Report Footer**.

5. To sort a column in the report, right-click the column you want sorted, then select either **Ascending** E or **Descending** F sort. Access will sort alphabetically for text fields or numerically for numeric fields.

6. To add sub-totals to your newly grouped report, right-click on the value in the field that you want to total, click the **Totals** button 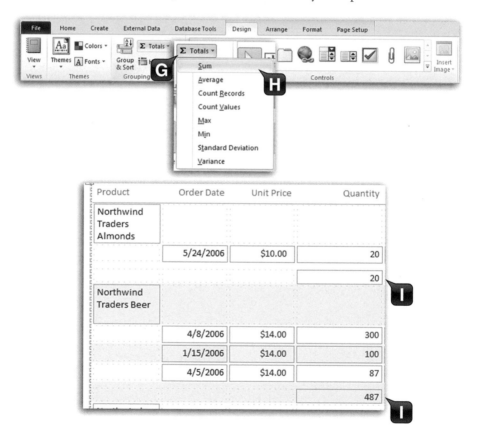 in the **Grouping & Totals** group on the **Design** tab.

7. Click the type of operation you would like to perform from the dropdown menu **H**. Access will add a group footer **I** with group totals, and a calculated text box at the bottom of the report that creates a grand total.

8. Click **Save** on the **File** tab, or hit **CTRL+S** to save your report.

Caution: In reports, you can only sort one field at a time using right-click. To sort on multiple fields, use the **Group, Sort, and Total** pane.

 Hot Tip: You can also specify grouping and sorting in the **Report Wizard** when you want to create more complicated reports than the simple, single-source report above.

11 Change Data Field Type in a Table or Query

Difficulty: ●○○○

PROBLEM You are looking for information in a particular field to provide dollar figures instead of text.

SOLUTION Assign a data type. You can assign different data types (such as dates, times, currency, numbers, or text) to fields. Assigning the field type as "currency" instead of "text" places a currency symbol, like a dollar sign ($), in front of your number and allows you to manipulate the numerical data.

Access 2010 has the following Data Types available:

Data Type	What It Is
Text	A series of characters, up to a maximum of 255.
Memo	Similar to text, with a maximum of 64,000 characters.
Number	Numeric data only. Some symbols can be used to designate positive (+) or negative (-) numbers, as well as decimal (.) points.
Currency	Primarily monetary numeric amounts, like US dollar, British pound, euro, yen, etc.
AutoNumber	A unique number for each record, either one greater than the value in the most recently created row or a random value. Access typically starts with the number 1.
Date/Time	Dates and times. Any date can be used between the years 100 and 9999.
Yes/No	This can be an operation using what "is" and what "is not." For example, "Yes/No," "True/False," "Male/Female," etc.
Object Linking and Embedding (OLE)	Other types of data can be embedded into your database, such as Microsoft Word documents, photos, audio, or other resources.
Hyperlink	A link that opens up a web page or directs the user to a certain file location.
Attachment	File(s) included as part of the record.
Lookup	A list of values obtained from either an existing table or query field or from a list you enter. You can permit users to assign multiple values to the field.
Rich Text	Text or a combination of text and numbers that can be formatted with color and font controls.
Calculated Field	The result of a calculation using other fields in the same table or query.

Step-by-Step

1. Open the table or query you want to work with in the object window.

2. If not already, switch your view to **Design** by clicking the **Design View** menu option **A** in the **View** dropdown menu in the **Views** group.

3. Click the field that you want to edit **B** in the **Data Type** column.

4. Click the dropdown **C**.

5. Select the new data type to assign to the field.

6. Review and specify any additional properties available for that data type in the **Field Properties** pane **D**. This is where you will set preferences for decimal points, integers, date options, etc.

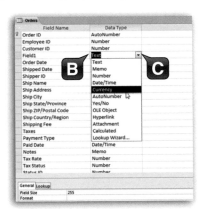

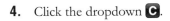

 Caution: While Access can change (with some exceptions) the data type even if there is already data in the table, you need to be careful. If you change the data type of existing data and it does not meet the criteria listed above, it deletes the data. For example, if text data is changed to number data, you lose any data with letters.

12 Create a New Expression Using the Expression Builder

Difficulty: ●●○○

PROBLEM You want to know how long it is taking your warehouse to ship products by calculating the difference between the date that the order was made and the date that the order was shipped.

SOLUTION Create an expression field using the Expression Builder. The expression builder in Access 2010 is a powerful dialog box that makes creating complex expression easier. In 2010, Microsoft added several new tools to offer even more help with expressions.

Step-by-Step

1. Open your query in the object window and switch to **Design** view.

2. In the empty column where you want your expression to go, right-click and select **Build** 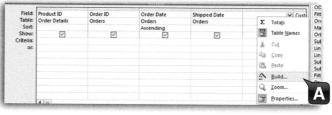 from the menu to open the **Expression Builder** dialog box:

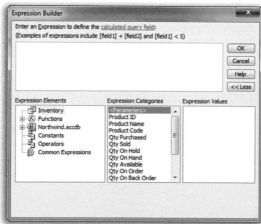

- The **Expression Elements** list 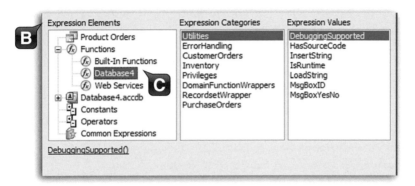 in the bottom left column shows all the types of elements that you can add to an expression. These include fields from your current query, functions, database items from the current database, constants, operators, and common expressions.

  - If you expand the sub-list under Functions, the options include built-in VBA functions, functions associated with the current database **C**, and functions available in Web Services.

- If you expand the sub-list under the name of your current database **D**, you will see a list of available objects. In this example **Tables**, **Queries**, **Forms**, and **Reports** are available. Selecting an object will open its available categories in the **Expression Categories** column **E**. Selecting an object will open a list of values for that object in the **Expression Values** column **F**.

CONTINUE

• The **Constants**, **Operators**, and **Common Expressions** options offer you built-in VBA constants, VBA operators, and a few common expressions for you to use as you build expressions.

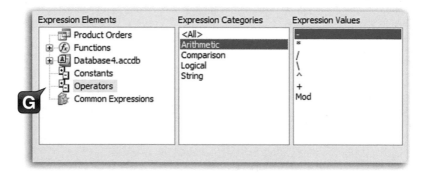

3. Build your expression by either typing in the top text box of the **Expression Builder** or by double clicking on the objects, elements, and functions in the **Expression Categories** and **Expression Values** columns.

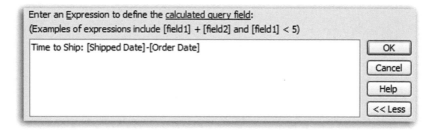

4. When your expression is complete, click **OK** to return to design view and apply your calculated field to the query .

	Order Date ▾	Shipped Date ▾	Time to Ship ▾	
	Product Orders			
30	1/15/2006	1/22/2006	7	Cc
30	1/15/2006	1/22/2006	7	Cc
31	1/20/2006	1/22/2006	2	Cc
31	1/20/2006	1/22/2006	2	Cc
31	1/20/2006	1/22/2006		Cc
32	1/22/2006	1/22/2006		
32	1/22/2006	1/22/2006	0	Cc
33	1/30/2006	1/31/2006	1	Cc
34	2/6/2006	2/7/2006	1	Cc
35	2/10/2006	2/12/2006	2	Cc
36	2/23/2006	2/25/2006	2	Cc

Hot Tip: When you type in the expression text box, Access IntelliSense will offer you pop up choices of functions and descriptions 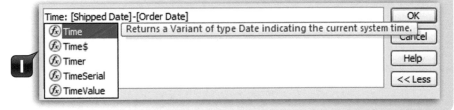. To quickly enter expressions, just type the first few letters of a function and then select the complete function name from the IntelliSense suggestions. This is not only quicker, but ensures that you will enter the function names and parameters correctly.

13 | Create a Web Database

What Is a Web Database?

In Access 2010, Microsoft provides a platform for you to create a Web database and share it on the Web using SharePoint. Access Services publishes your database to SharePoint, and SharePoint users can access the database in a web browser. You can then control permissions for users of your database. Microsoft is now offering an Internet-facing, hosted SharePoint solution so you can publish your database the Internet or to your own intranet.

Once your web database is published, forms, reports and most macros will run inside the browser, which reduces screen refresh events. Queries and data macros will run on the SharePoint server to reduce network traffic.

A Web database offers you unique opportunities to share your information with colleagues who may work in other locations or with customers who regularly interact with your data. You can share data population chores by creating forms for users to input their own data from wherever they are, rather than requiring them to travel onsite. By publishing your data to the Internet, you can work on the database from anywhere that has Internet access.

As with any public-facing platform, you will need to be conscientious of security issues. Any time your information is opened for public access, you run the risk of attacks from malicious users. Even with passwords and protections in place, no public data is completely secure. Evaluate the sensitivity of your data and research security risks thoroughly before you decide what information to publish.

What Is Different?

While you will still design and populate your database in Access, several features are not available in a Web database that you may have come to expect in your desktop database. Union queries, Crosstab queries, Overlapping controls on form, Table relationships, conditional formatting and various macro actions and expressions are desktop-database-only features. Consider using the **Blank Web Database** template located in the **Available Templates** section of the **New** tab in the backstage view to get used to Web database design.

Another significant difference is the need to create a Navigation Form. This is done from the Create tab in the **Forms** group. Users will not see the Access Navigation Pan in their web browser, so you must provide them links to the tables, queries, and forms that they have permission to access. A Navigation

form will be displayed when a user opens your application in their web browser.

Setting Permissions

Controlling access to your database is an important part of supporting an online resource. The integrity, confidentiality, and privacy of your data is dependent upon making your site secure. Permissions are managed through SharePoint groups or at the SharePoint site collection level. You will need to become very familiar with the security levels and options for your database's site before you publish.

Publishing and Synchronizing Your Web Database

When your database is ready to share, you will need to publish it to SharePoint for your users to begin accessing it. The publishing process begins on the **Save & Publish** tab in the backstage view. Click **Publish to Access Services** to open the **Access Services Overview** pane. From here you will be able to run the **Compatibility Checker** to make sure that your database will publish correctly or to check if you need to fix any issues first.

You will next need to fill in information about where your database is going to be served from. You will need to know the web address of the SharePoint server where you want your database published. (And you will need a SharePoint account!) Click **Publish to Access Services** to complete publishing.

Once your database is in use, you will find times when you need to make changes or take a database offline for an amount of time. Synchronizing will resolve differences between the database file on your desktop and the one on the SharePoint site. When you are ready to synchronize, open the backstage view and click **Sync All**.

14 Document a Database

When you initially build a database, the structure is fresh on your mind, and it is easy to think that you will remember how all of the elements are organized. However, as the database grows, it may become overwhelmingly large and complicated. Documenting the structure assists with managing and maintaining the database.

Access creates reports to document the database structure that can be saved or printed. These reports illustrate the design and properties of the objects in your database. Run the database documenter to structure information in case of a problem and to allow others to see the layout of the database objects clearly.

Step-by-Step

1. Close all Access object windows except for your main database window.

2. Click on the **Database Tools** tab **A**.

3. In the **Analyze** group, click on **Database Documenter** **B**.

4. The **Documenter** dialog box opens **C**, displaying multiple tabs.

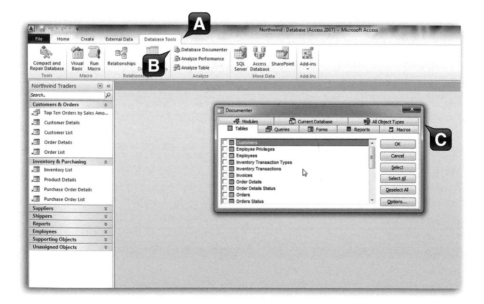

5. Click the tab that contains the object(s) you want to document.

6. Click the checkbox next to an object to select it. You can use the **Select All** or **Deselect All** buttons to control multiple checkboxes at once.

7. Click the **OK** button.

8. The report details the properties of the selected object(s) **D**.

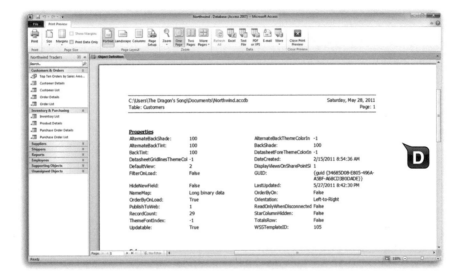

Hot Tip: Choose one object at a time. The report may be unmanageably long if you document every element of the database at once.

15 Customize Form Header

Difficulty: ●○○○

PROBLEM Your marketing director just released a new company logo and branding model. In an effort to push this brand to all employees, marketing has asked that everyone incorporate this branding into all department documentation. You generate forms that are filled out by employees throughout your organization.

SOLUTION Customize your form header. You can add customized branding or your company logo to your form to add a more professional, polished look.

Step-by-Step

1. Open the form you want to work with in the object window.

2. If you are not already in **Design** view, click the **Design** view menu option **A** in the **View** dropdown menu in the **Views** group. The **Form Design Tools** contextual tab will appear.

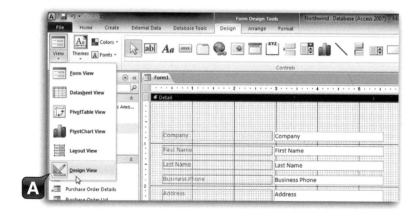

3. Click on the existing header textbox **B**. If one does not already exist, click on the **Title** button **C** in the **Header/Footer** group in the **Design** tab to add a **Form Header**.

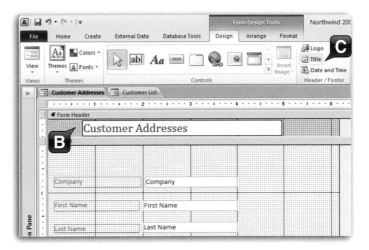

4. Click and drag to adjust the box to the desired width and height. Add or change the title text in the label box as needed.

5. You can manipulate the font size, type, color, and style by using the buttons in the **Font** group **D** on the **Format** tab.

6. You can add an image into the header by clicking on the **Logo** button 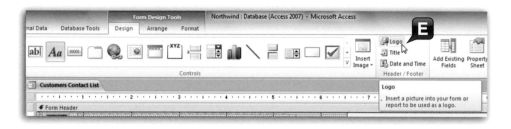 in the **Header/Footer** group on the **Design** tab to launch the **Insert Picture** dialog box. Browse to the image you want to insert, then click **OK**.

7. You can add a background color by right-clicking anywhere in the header textbox and selecting **Fill/Back Color F** and choosing a color from the palette **G**.

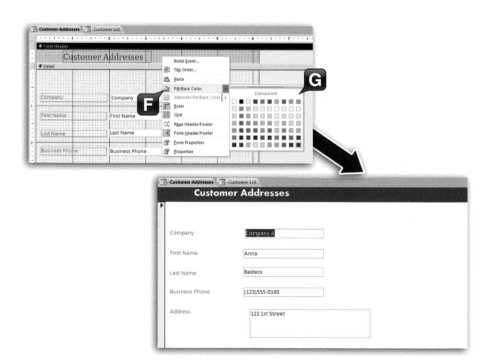

Quickest Click: Use **Controls** (textbox, radio buttons, labels, etc.) to quickly add design features to your form. When you click on any control in the **Controls** group **H** on the **Design** tab, the mouse will change the cursor to a picture of the tool you are using. To return to a regular select arrow, either click the **Escape (ESC)** button on your keyboard or click the **Select** button **I** in your **Control** group.

16 Create and Use Yes/No Fields

Difficulty: ●●○○

PROBLEM You would like to add a way for you to know if a project stored in your database is "open" or "closed."

SOLUTION Create a Yes/No field. In a table, one of the data type options is Yes/No. This is commonly used for True/False values in your database. Displayed as a checkbox, this data type is useful when tracking any type of True/False data.

Add a field called "Status" to your table. If the answer is no and the order remains open, the box will remain unchecked. If the answer is yes, the box is checked and the order is closed.

See Also: Create a New Table; Change Data Field Type in a Table or Query

Step-by-Step

Add the Yes/No Data Type into Table

1. Open the table you want to work with in the object window.

2. If you are not already in **Design** view, click the **Design View** menu option in the **View** dropdown menu in the **Views** group.

3. Create a new field name **A**.

4. In the **Data Type** field, click the dropdown and select **Yes/No** **B**.

5. Enter your data (indicating a True/False state) in this field by checking the check box or leaving it blank.

▲ Step-by-Step

Query Results Using 1/0

1. Open an existing query or create a new one using the table with the **Yes/No** field.

2. Add the **Yes/No** field (Status) from the Customer's table to your query **C**.

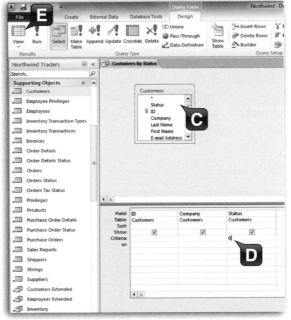

3. In the criteria field textbox **D**, type a **1** (indicating yes or true) or a **0** (indicating no or false).

4. Your results will display data based on the criteria you specified to pull (either **1** [yes] or **0** [no]). For example, if you selected **1** for this data type, to indicate you wanted to see open projects only, then you will retrieve only data with rows of open projects.

5. Click the **View E** button in the **Results** group of the **Design** tab to see the query results.

> **Hot Tip:** This field is especially functional through 1/0 in a query. You can select criteria to 1 (checked) or 0 (unchecked) to pull Yes/No information and select only specific rows of data for your query results.

STOP

17 | Rename a Field in a Form

Difficulty: ●○○○

PROBLEM Your current customer contact form has a field called "Customer," which indicates the name of the customer. However, several departments use the term customer to refer to "Customer Type" (such as Full Service Customer) or "Customer Number" (such as 1234). To be perfectly clear about what information you are asking for in this field, you want to change the field name from "Customer" to "Company Name."

SOLUTION Rename the field. Sometimes a field in a current report no longer makes sense, or it is not applicable to those viewing the form. Editing or renaming a field in a report is useful if you need to present existing report information in a more applicable or clear manner.

Step-by-Step

1. Open the form you want to work with in the object window.

2. If you are not already in **Design** view, click the **Design** view menu option in the **View** dropdown menu in the **Views** group. The **Form Design Tools** contextual tab will appear.

3. Select and highlight the field name you want to edit **A**.

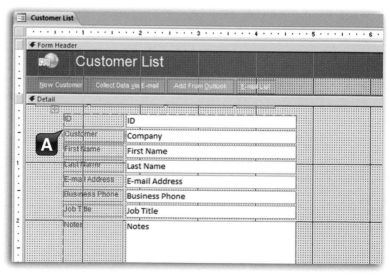

5. Type in the new name over the old text **B**.

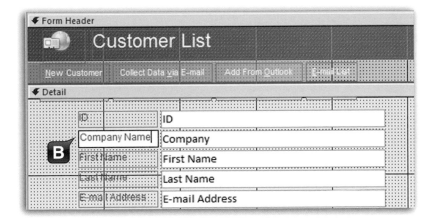

6. Click **Save** on the **File** tab, or hit **CTRL+S** to save your form.

7. Return to **Form View** by selecting **Form View** from the **View** dropdown menu on the **Home** tab.

8. Verify that your field name now appears correctly **C**.

STOP

18 Change Field Properties

Difficulty: ●●○○

PROBLEM Your table stores all employees' birth dates as mm/dd/yy. You want to run a query to pull all birthdays for the month to post up on the Birthday Board, but you don't want to include the year.

SOLUTION Set the property format. Every field in a database has properties associated with it, which allows you to customize the way the data is stored. These properties can eliminate data entry errors and make it easier for the user to keep the field input consistent. Field properties can be changed in a table, query, form, or report. You can set the property format in the query to mm/dd without changing this information in your table.

Step-by-Step

1. Open a **Table**, **Query**, **Form**, or **Report** you want to work with in the object window.

2. If you are not already in **Design** view, click the **Design** view menu option in the **View** dropdown menu in the **Views** group.

3. Click on the row that contains the field with the properties you want to change **A**. The **Field Properties** window **B** below the object window will display the properties for that field.

4. Click on the name of the property you want to change .

5. Change the properties by following one or more of these steps:

- Type a new value for the property.
- Click the dropdown **D** and choose a new value from a list

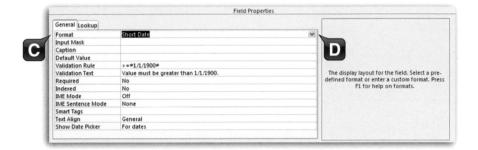

- Click the **Build** button **E** to open the **Expression Builder**.

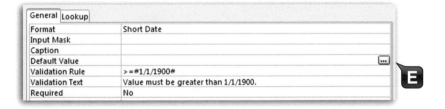

Bright Idea: There are field properties in **Tables**, **Queries**, **Forms**, and **Reports**. The field properties displayed change depending on which object you are working in. If you right-click any field on any object, you see all the available properties, such as field height, font information, style information, etc.

19 | Sorting Table or Query Data

Difficulty: ●○○○

PROBLEM The records for your mailing list database were entered over the course of several months in groups as you gathered leads at trade shows. You would like a way to organize your table in a way that makes it easier to see where your leads tend to live and what type of products they might buy from you.

SOLUTION Sort your information.

Step-by-Step

1. Open the table or query you want to sort in the object window in **Datasheet** view.

2. To sort by a single field at a time, click the dropdown arrow to the right of the field title you wish to sort **A**.

3. Click Ascending or Descending sort:

   • Smallest to Largest or Largest to Smallest – applies to numeric values

   • Oldest to Newest or Newest to Oldest – applies to date values

   • A to Z or Z to A – applies to text values

   The column will be reordered according to your choice, and a small arrow **B** will appear to the right of the field name, next to the dropdown arrow. Upward indicates an ascending sort; downward arrow indicates a descending sort. ▲

4. To add a second sort function, select a second field column and repeat steps 2-3. Access will complete the new sort **C** and re-order your first column as needed to do so **D**. Sort order is determined by the order that the sorts are added, with the last sort becoming the primary sort.

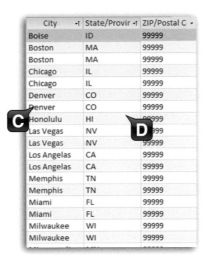

5. To clear all sorts from a table or query, click the **Remove Sort** button **E** in the **Sort & Filter** group on the **Home** tab.

CONTINUE

6. To sort more than one field at the same time, hold the shift key and click all the fields you want sorted. They must be next to each other; you can't group sort non-contiguous fields.

7. Click the **Ascending**  or the **Descending** button in the **Sort & Filter** group on the **Home** tab.

8. Your selection will sort the leftmost field first, then sort the next field to the right within that search, and so on.

Compare the difference: The first example was sorted in two steps by selecting the Last Name field column first, clicking **Ascending**, clicking the First Name Column and clicking **Ascending** in sequence. The second example sorted both field columns at once **G**. Notice that customers with the same last name were sorted by last name first, then by first name **I**.

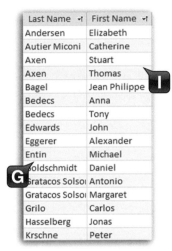

9. Click **Remove Sort** to return the table or query to the original state. Click **Save** on the **File** tab or hit **CTRL+S** to save the new table layout.

> **Caution:** Access sorts differently depending on the data type of the field. It will sort text character by character from left to right, but treat numeric data as a single value. This can be confusing if a field is saving figures as text, as is common with phone numbers and zip codes, for example. Make sure your data types are correct for the type of sorting and filtering you will need.

Original	Sorted as Text	Sorted as Number
1	1	1
1234	11	3
23	12	4
3	1234	11
11	22	12
22	23	22
12	3	23
4	4	1234

STOP

20 | Use Filters on a Table or Query

Difficulty: ●●○○

PROBLEM You need to find a list of employees in your Employee Information Database started with the organization prior to January 1, 2007.

SOLUTION Use filters to trim your data and show only what you need at the time. When you filter data, you use specific criteria to tell Access what you want to see. After applying a filter, you will only see the records that pass through. In this case, you see a list of employees who started before January 1 of 2007. The rest of your data is available but hidden. If you remove the filter, the rest of your data displays. You can use filters on records in forms, reports, queries, or datasheets. Filters can also be used to print only certain records from a report, table, or query.

> **What Microsoft Calls It:** Filtering Table Records

Step-by-Step

Open the form, report, query, or table that contains the records you wish to filter. Follow the steps below according to your needs and the type of data you filter (date, text, number, etc.).

Applying a Common Filter

A **Common Filter** is a collection of the most used filters in Microsoft Access. These include things like "equal to," "greater than," and others for numerical data. For text data, common filters include things like "contains," "ends with," and "begins with." For dates, common filters include "before" and "after."

In this example, in the Orders table, we want to find all orders that were placed prior to January 1, 2007.

1. Click on any field in the column displaying the data you wish to filter **A**. In this case click on a field in the Order Date column.

2. Click the **Filter** button on the **Home** tab **B**. A fly out menu will appear.

3. Click on **Date Filters** **C** in the **Filter** menu and select the appropriate filter type.

4. For this example, you would choose **Before...** **D**. The **Custom Filter** dialog box will open.

5. Fill in the date that you want to filter by in the **Order Date is on or before** text box **E**. ⚠

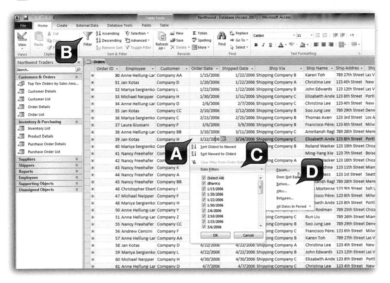

6. Click the **OK** button. A filter icon **F** will appear in the column heading of the fields that have a filter applied.

7. To go back and forth between filtered and unfiltered data, click on the **Toggle Filter** button **G** in the **Sort & Filter** group on the **Home** tab. To remove a filter, click on the filter icon in the column heading, then select **Clear filter from (column name) H**.

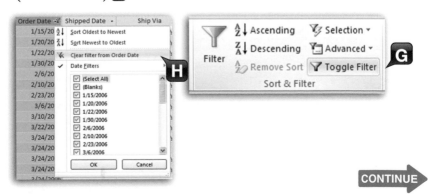

CONTINUE

Step-by-Step

Filter by Selection

Filtering by selection allows you to filter all the records in a table that matches the specific value you have selected in a single row. You can filter by date (same month only, for example), number, or text, simply by selecting the field that has the value you want to match. If you want to view all of the orders for only 10 units, you would select the field with a unit number of 10 and filter by selection based on that value.

1. Select value from your data that you wish to filter by **I**.

2. Click the **Selection J** arrow in your **Home** tab. The dropdown menu displays the appropriate filter options available for the selection. In this example, **Equals 10** was selected.

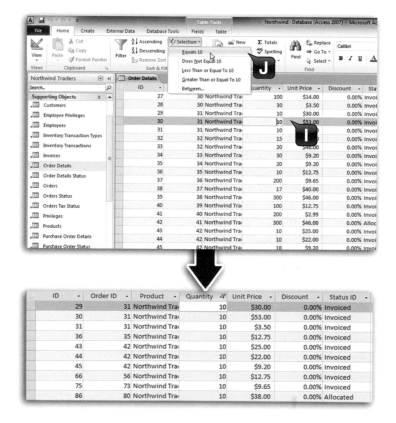

Option: Filtering may not be the best option when looking for certain information, such as high or low values, unique values, or duplicates. In such cases, you may want to use a query instead.

Hot Tip: Certain characters, such as *****, **%**, and **?** have a special meaning when specified in a filter textbox. To see the complete list and their meanings, see **Appendix B.**

Caution: The **Before…** filter type filters the data *on* and before that date. Therefore, in this example, to view orders placed prior to 6/1/2006, the date that needs to be entered into this dialog box is 5/31/2006 **K**.

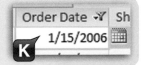

Bright Idea: Once you apply a filter to your data, you might decide that you want to use it in a form or report. You can use the buttons on the **Create** tab of the **Ribbon**. First, filter the datasheet, and select the type of object you want to create. The report or form will use the filtered data.

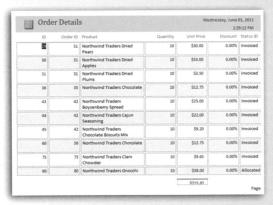

21 | Use Advanced Options for Filters

Difficulty: ●●○○

PROBLEM You want to find employees who both started before January 1, 2007 and opted out of the company's medical benefits.

SOLUTION **Filter by Form** and **Advanced Filter/Sort** are two advanced-level filter functions available in Access 2010. **Filter by Form** is used when filtering data with more than one criterion. An **Advanced Filter/Sort** works like a simple query. It finds and sorts data from one table.

 What Microsoft Calls It: Filtering Table Records

 **Step-by-Step**

Filter by Form

1. Open the form, report, query, or table that contains the records you wish to filter.

2. Click the **Advanced** dropdown button **A** in the **Sort & Filter** group on the **Home** tab.

3. Select **Filter by Form** **B**. This opens a form that looks like a single row of the table you are filtering **C**.

4. Click in any field and then select the value you want to filter by from the dropdown menu **D**. These values will depend on the type of data stored in the field. Repeat as needed to narrow your results further. Only the records that match *all* of the criteria you have specified will be displayed.

5. If you want broader results, click the **OR** tab at the bottom of the object window to add criteria as an OR statement. Select additional values from the dropdown options. Repeat as needed.

6. To display the filtered results, click the **Toggle Filter** button **E** in the **Sort & Filter** ribbon of the Home tab.

7. Your results display in the form **F**.

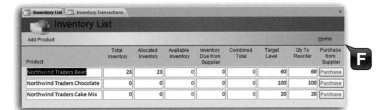

Step-by-Step

Advanced Filter/Sort

1. Open the form, report, query, or table that contains the records you wish to filter.

2. Click the **Advanced** dropdown button **G** in the **Sort & Filter** group on the **Home** tab.

3. Select **Advanced Filter/Sort** **H** from the menu to open the **Query Design View** page with your table(s) already added **I**.

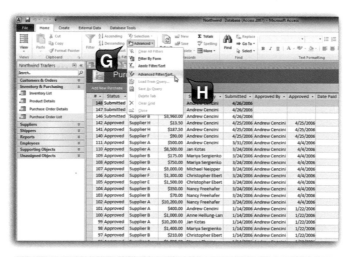

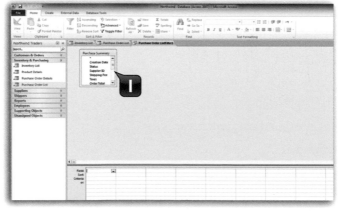

4. Add the fields you want to filter by to the grid by clicking in the **Field** row and selecting the field's name from the dropdown menu 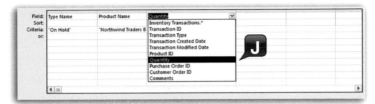. Specify a **Sort** order in the same way **K**.

5. Specify the criterion to filter on by clicking on the **Criteria** row **L** and entering your expression.

6. Click the **Toggle Filter** button to view your results.

 Hot Tip: Use the expression builder to create the expressions for your advanced filters. Right-click on the **Criteria** row of the field you need an expression. Choose the **Build** menu option to launch the **Expression Builder** dialog box.

 STOP

22 Compare Two Tables and Search for Differences

Difficulty: ●●○○

PROBLEM Your boss asks you to review customers who have not made any orders lately. You want to approach these clients with a special offer to encourage them to buy from you again.

SOLUTION To find records in one table that do not have corresponding records in another table, create a **Find Unmatched Records** query. To obtain this information quickly, query your Customers table to find clients who do not match up with clients on the Orders table.

Step-by-Step

1. Click the **Create** tab **A**.

2. Click the **Query Wizard** button **B** in the **Queries** group to open the **New Query** dialog box.

3. Click **Find Unmatched Query Wizard** **C**.

4. Click the **OK** button.

5. Click the table in which you want to find unmatched records **D**.

6. Click the **Next** button.

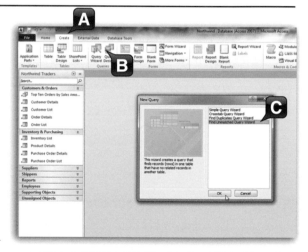

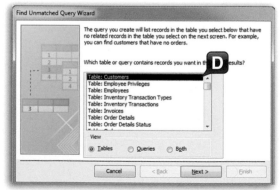

7. Click the table or query that holds the related records you are looking for 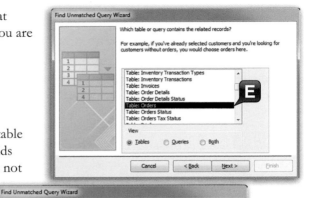.

8. Click the **Next** button.

9. The left and right panes display the fields for each table selected. The matching fields are highlighted. If they are not already highlighted, click the match button **F**, which displays the matched fields.

10. Click the **Next** button.

11. Click the name(s) of the field(s) you want to display in your query results **G**. Click ▷ to add a single field to the **Selected field**s pane **H**, or click ▷▷ to add all fields at once.

12. Click the **Next** button.

13. Name your query **I**. Access automatically assigns a name if you do not type one in.

14. Click the **Finish** button.

23 Aggregate Query Data

Difficulty: ●○○○

PROBLEM You have a query that displays sales orders by product for each sales team member. The datasheet shows you how much each sales team member sold, but you would like a quick way to view your total bottom line and learn the totals sales amounts per sales team member.

SOLUTION Add a Total row to your query. A Total row is a row at the bottom of your datasheet that displays running and grand totals of the data in your field.

> 💬 **What Microsoft Calls It:** Add a Total Row, Create a Totals Query

Step-by-Step

1. Open the query you want to modify in the object window.

2. Click the **Totals** button **A** in the **Records** group on the **Home** tab. A new row at the bottom of the datasheet will appear with the row heading of **Total B**.

3. Click any cell in the **Total** row that you want a total for. A dropdown arrow **C** will appear.

4. Click the dropdown arrow to view the available aggregate functions **D**:
   - **Sum**: Totals the values in the field. Use with **Number**, **Decimal**, and **Currency** data types.
   - **Average**: Averages the values by applying the formula "sum divided by count." The field must contain numeric, currency, or date/time data. The function ignores null values.
   - **Count**: Counts the number of instances of a value. Use with All data types except complex repeating scalar data.

- **Maximum**: Calculates the largest numeric value, the latest date, or the last alphabetical value for text values. Use with **Number**, **Decimal**, **Currency**, and **Date/Time** data types.
- **Minimum**: Calculates the smallest numeric value, the earliest date, or the first alphabetical value for text values. Use with **Number**, **Decimal**, **Currency**, and **Date/Time** data types.
- **Variance**: Measures the statistical variance of all values in the field. Can only use this function on numeric and currency data.

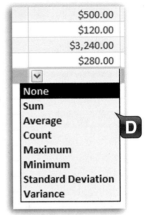

You will only be offered those functions that apply to the type of data stored in the field. Choose the function you want to apply to the cell. The footer will display the results of the function you have chosen **E**.

- **Standard Deviation**: Measures how widely values are dispersed from an average value (a mean). Use with **Number**, **Decimal**, and **Currency** data types.

5. Click **Save** on the **File** tab or hit **CTRL+S** to save your query.

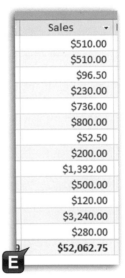

24 | Create a Calculation in a Query Field

Difficulty: ●●○○

PROBLEM You manage your small business inventory using Access. Until today, you were entering in a customer's total bill price. However, you want to start viewing the sales tax associated with each purchase.

SOLUTION Create a calculated field. Access performs very simple or very complex mathematical equations in a database. This saves time because you do not have to manually calculate items, and it is virtually error-free as long as the initial values and equations are written correctly. A calculation automatically creates the sales tax amount every time.

See Also: Create a New Expression Using the Expression Builder

Step-by-Step

1. Open the query you want in the **Object Window**, then click the **View** button in the **Views** group on the **Home** tab and select **Design** view from the dropdown menu.

2. In an empty column of the **Design Grid** below the object window, type a unique, new field name into the **Field** row, followed by a colon, the field name, and an expression that performs the calculation you want to perform . For example: Taxes: [Product Total Amount]*.06.

   In this example, the new field name is **Taxes**. It pulls the **Product Total Amount** field and multiplies it (*) by 6% sales tax (.06).

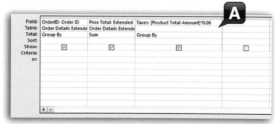

3. To view your query results with your calculated field, click the **Run** button **B** in the **Results** group on the **Design** tab.

OrderID	Price Total	Taxes
30	$1,505.00	$90.30
31	$865.00	$51.90
32	$1,190.00	$71.40
33	$276.00	$16.56
34	$184.00	$11.04
35	$127.50	$7.65
36	$1,930.00	$115.80
37	$680.00	$40.80
38	$13,800.00	$828.00
39	$1,275.00	$76.50
40	$598.00	$35.88
41	$13,800.00	$828.00
42	$562.00	$33.72
43	$219.50	$13.17
44	$1,674.75	$100.49

STOP

25 | Create a Query that Prompts Users for Search Criteria

Difficulty: ●●○○

PROBLEM You run a monthly query to pull all customer appointments for that month. Using a single query instead of twelve different ones would be easier and more efficient.

SOLUTION A parameter query prompts the user for value(s) every time it runs. This means that you can change the selection criteria for the query without making a change in the query design grid. The value that the query asks for can be text, a date, a number, or Yes/No. First, create one parameter query. Specify the date as a parameter value with a data type integer that can be changed each time you run the query.

Step-by-Step

---

1. Open the query you want in the **Object Window**, then click the **View** button in the **Views** group on the **Home** tab and select **Design View** from the dropdown menu **A**.

2. Under the field name you wish to create the parameter for, enter the parameter on the **Criteria** row in the following format: [Parameter Name]. *Note: The parameter name should not match one of your table field names* **B**.

3. Use the following steps to define the data type for the criteria so Access will perform data validation on the user's input. This means if the query asks for a date, the user will only be able to enter a date.
   a. Click the **Parameters** button **C** in the **Show/Hide** group of the **Design** tab to open the **Query Parameters** dialog box.

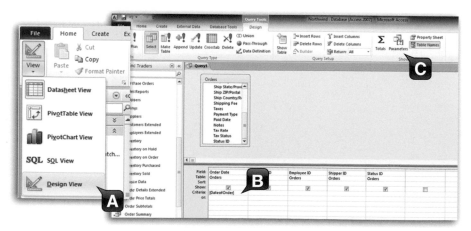

b. Type the name of the parameter that you want to validate in the **Parameter** column **D**.

c. Select a data type from the dropdown options in the **Data Type** column **E**. The data type matches the type of data that the parameter requests. For example, **Currency** for a dollar value, **Date/Time** for a date or time, or **Text** for text. *Note: Step 3 actions can be repeated to include as many parameters as you want to use.*

4. Click the **OK** button to return to **Design** view. To save your query, click **Save** in the **File** tab or type **CTRL+S**.

5. To run your query with parameters, click the **Run** button **F** in the **Results** group on the **Design** tab. An **Enter Parameter Value** dialog box will open with the name of the parameter. Type your value into the text box, then click **OK** to view your results. ◊

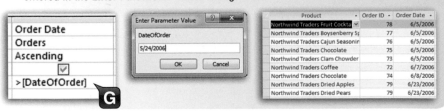

Hot Tip: The parameters don't have to be exact match parameters. For example, typing **>[DateOfOrder] G** in the **Criteria** row pulls any record with a date after the date entered in the **Enter Parameter Value** dialog box.

STOP

26 | Make a Crosstab Query

Difficulty: ●●○○

PROBLEM You want to look at total sales and compare it with a salesperson's name and sales quarter.

SOLUTION Use a Crosstab Query to display the results in an easy-to-read format, with the salesperson's name on the left, the quarters across the top, and the results in between. Crosstab Queries help you analyze data in your tables by summarizing or calculating how many records contain certain combinations of values. In other words, crosstab queries allow you to easily calculate results in a spreadsheet format (by row and column).

See Also: Create a PivotTable View for a Query

Step-by-Step

Create a Crosstab Query

1. Click the **Create** tab **A**.

2. Click the **Query Wizard B** to open the **New Query** dialog box.

3. Select **Crosstab Query Wizard C**.

4. Click the **OK** button to launch the **Crosstab Query Wizard**.

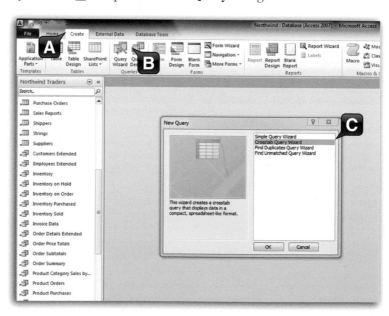

5. Select the table or query that provides the values for your crosstab query 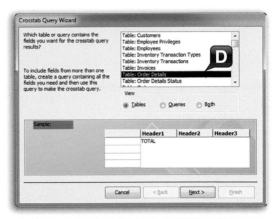.

6. Click the **Next** button.

7. Select a field from the **Available Fields** list to provide values for the row headings 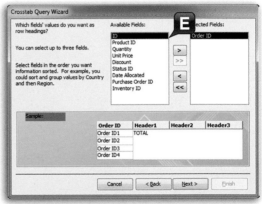.

8. Click the right arrow button to move the fields you select to the **Selected Fields** list.

9. Click the **Next** button.

10. Click the field where you will obtain values for the column headings 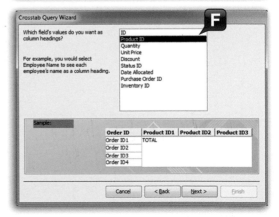.

11. Click the **Next** button.

Make a Crosstab Query **75**

12. Click the field where you will obtain values for the data area (body) of the **Crosstab Query** **G**.

13. Click the summary calculation to be performed on the values in the data area **H**.

14. Click the **Next** button.

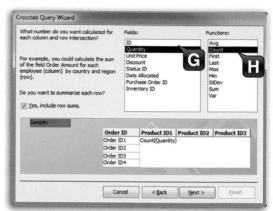

15. Type a name for the query in the **What do you want to name your query?** text box **I**. Access automatically assigns a generic name if based off an already existing named file.

16. Click the **Finish** button **J**.

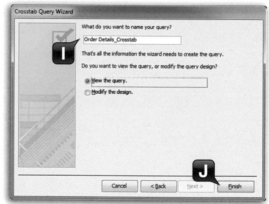

Hot Tip: You can add up to three fields on the left to increase groupings like Years and Months or Department and Employee name.

 Caution: For each column and row intersection, you can have only one value. In other words, you cannot calculate the total sales *and* number of items sold in one query. If you need to build a query with more than one value field, you can build a standard select query and use the **Pivot Table View**.

27 Create a Query that Searches by Specified Parts of Dates

Difficulty: ●●●○

PROBLEM You need to know what month or year a particular event falls on, or you are reviewing financial information and want to know the quarter in which certain events occurred.

SOLUTION Use a **DatePart** function. **DatePart** is a function that returns a number from a specific part of the date field.

 What Microsoft Calls It: DatePart function

Step-by-Step

1. Open the query you want to work with in the object window.

2. If not already in **Design** view, click the **Design** view menu option in the **View** dropdown menu in the **Views** group.

3. In the **Design Grid,** click on an empty cell in the **Field** row .

4. Enter your **DatePart** function by typing the following syntax **B**:

   - **DatePart("setting",[NameofDateField])**
   - **Setting** refers to one of the codes for **DatePart** (see table).
   - **NameofDateField** refers to the field name in your table that contains the date.

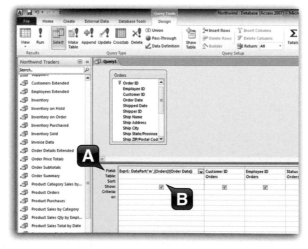

Setting	Description
yyyy	Year
q	Quarter
m	Month
y	Day of year
d	Day
w	Weekday
ww	Week
h	Hour
n	Minute
s	Second

4. Click the **Save** button on the **File** tab or type **CTRL+S** to save your query.

5. Click the **Run** button **C** in the **Results** group of the **Design** tab.

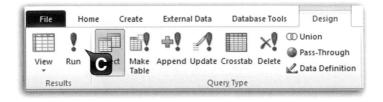

28 Create Charts and Graphs

Difficulty: ●●○○

PROBLEM You manage a sales team, and your staff is currently organized with one salesperson per region. Over the last year, your customer base has shifted significantly, and your northern region now holds over 50 percent of the customer base. You want to use this information as part of supporting documentation to restructure your department. You can create a general report that shows customer name and region, but it might take verbal or written explanation to paint the whole picture.

SOLUTION Create a chart. Create a pie chart that shows a large sector of these northern clients compared to the small pie pieces for the other regions. This visual description provides a clear message without any additional information.

Step-by-Step

1. Click the **Create** tab **A** and click on the **Blank Form** button **B** in the **Forms** group, or open an existing or new report.

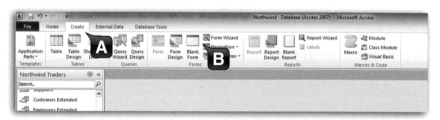

2. Open the **Design View** in the **Views** group of the **Format** or **Home** tab.

3. On the **Design tab**, click on the **Insert Chart** button **C** in the **Control** group to open the **Chart Wizard** dialog box.

4. In your blank form, click and drag the cursor to define the chart's area. This area can be edited later to be smaller or larger.

5. In the **Chart Wizard** dialog box, select the radio button **D** to display the database tables, queries, or both in the **Which table or query would you like to use to create your chart?** pane.

6. Click the table or query that contains the data you want to use to create your chart **E**.

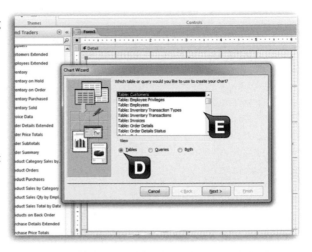

7. Click the **Next** button.

8. Select the field(s) that you want on your chart in the **Available Fields** box. Click the **Add** button ▶ to move them to the **Fields for Chart** box.

9. Click the **Next** button.

10. Select the type of chart you want to use to display your data **F**.

11. Click the **Next** button.

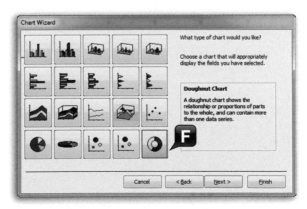

12. Evaluate the preview of your chart on the left-hand side of the dialog box. If you want to select a different chart, click the **Back** button. If you want to continue, click the **Next** button.

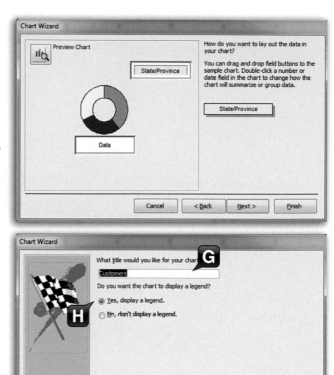

13. Enter a title for your chart **G** and select the radio button **H** to instruct Access whether or not you want a legend for your chart. Legends are useful for easy analysis of the data, especially when you have long heading names.

14. Click the **Finish** button.

Option: Add a chart or graph to an existing open report by either copying and pasting a chart that currently exists or by creating a new one using the Wizard.

Hot Tip: If your selected fields are dates or numbers, you can double-click on the box **I** to edit the way that data will display on your chart.

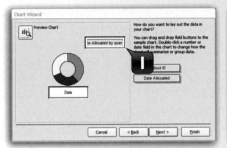
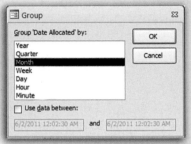

29 Format Charts and Graphs

Difficulty: ●○○○

PROBLEM You provided your manager with a chart of your department's revenue for the quarter in a bar chart format. When she reviews it, she decides that she likes the format, but wants to change the colors to reflect the corporate branding and remove the legend.

SOLUTION When you want to change the layout, colors, fonts, and display of your chart or graph, you can format or edit it using the Microsoft Graph tool. You can edit the layout of your chart by using the format tools.

 What Microsoft Calls It: Microsoft Graph

Step-by-Step

1. Open the chart that you want to format or edit in **Design View**, or create a new chart using the **Chart Wizard**. 🔥

2. Double-click on the chart **A** to open the editing toolbar.

3. On the **Menu** bar, click **Chart** and select **Chart Options** **B**.

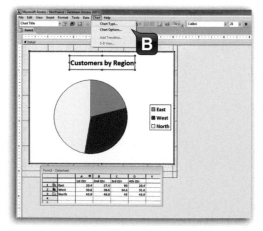

4. In the **Chart Options** dialog box 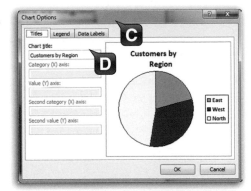, you can edit the title of your chart **D**, change the placement or availability of your legend **E**, and add data labels to your chart **F**.

5. Click **OK** to apply your changes.

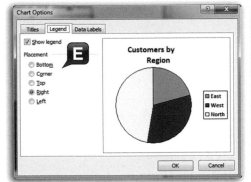

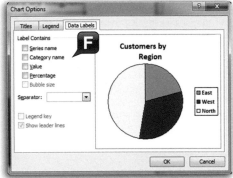

Bright idea: Access shows you what these changes will look like in the preview box before you approve the changes.

Hot Tip: You can edit any area of your chart by double-clicking that section while in the Microsoft Graph editing tool.

STOP

30 | Create a PivotTable View for a Query

Difficulty: ●●●○

PROBLEM You have a large database of regional sales information. You would like to analyze the data in such a way as to quickly learn your top performing regions and sales team members. Creating a query for each slice of the data that you want is time consuming and still difficult to compare. You need a way to generate a view that lets you change how you are viewing the data.

SOLUTION Create a PivotTable View. A PivotTable is an interactive table that combines large amounts of data. You can interchange rows and columns to view different interpretations of your information, and you can narrow in on specific areas of detail. Use a PivotTable when you have long lists of figures to sum and you want to analyze different aspects of each figure or filter out figures you don't need. You can also create PivotTable views for queries, tables, and forms.

Step-by-Step

1. Open the query you want to make a **PivotTable** view from in the **Object Window.**

2. Click the **View** button in the **Views** group on the **Home** tab. Click **PivotTable View A**. A blank **PivotTable B** will open in the **Object Window** and the **PivotTable Field List** dialog box **C** will open. 🔥

3. In the **PivotTable Field List** dialog box, click on the field you want to add to the **Row Fields**, then select **Row Area D** from the dropdown list at the bottom of the **PivotTable Field List** dialog box.

4. Click **Add to E**. The field data **F** will appear in the object window in the **Drop Row Fields Here** area. ⚡

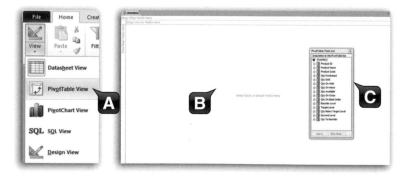

5. Click on the field you want to add to the **Column Fields**, then select **Column Area** 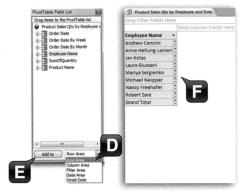 from the dropdown list at the bottom of the **PivotTable Field List** dialog box.

6. Click **Add to**. The field data **H** will appear in the **Object Window** in the **Drop Column Fields Here** area.

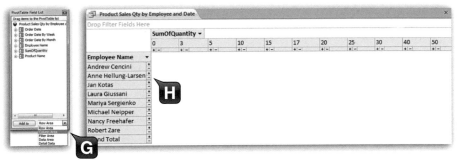

7. To add detail fields—those that make up the detail cells of the PivotTable—click on the field you want to add, then select **Detail Data** **I** from the dropdown list at the bottom of the **PivotTable Field List** dialog box.

8. Click **Add to**. The field data **J** will appear in the **Object Window** in the **Drop Column Fields Here** area. Repeat for each field needed.

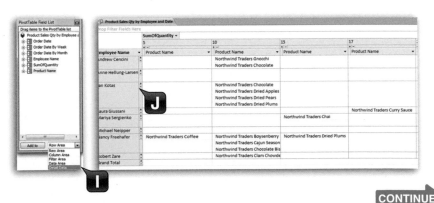

CONTINUE

Filter fields are optional, but they allow you to filter the entire **PivotTable** by the values of your choosing. If you wish to add a filter field, click on the field you want to filter by in the **PivotTable Field List** dialog box, then select **Filter Area** **K** from the dropdown list at the bottom of the dialog box.

9. Click **Add to**. The field data **L** will appear in the **Object Window** in the **Drop Column Fields Here** area. Repeat for each filter as needed.

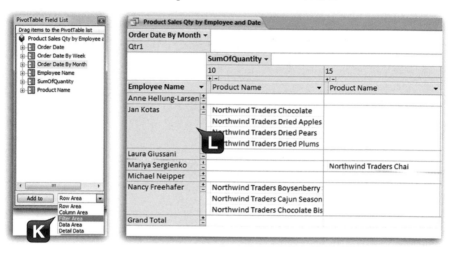

10. If you want to move a field to another place in the **PivotTable**, select the field, then click the **Move Field** button **M** in the **Active Field** group on the **Design** tab. Choose the menu option that fits your destination. ✸

11. To delete a field from the PivotTable view, click on the name of the field you want to delete, then click **Remove Field**  in the **Active Field** group on the **Design** tab under the **PivotTable Tools** contextual tab. This deletes the field from the *view* only. The underlying data source is still available.

12. Click **Save** on the **File** tab or hit **CTRL + S** to save your **PivotTable** view for the query.

 Hot Tip: If you don't see the **PivotTable Field List** dialog box when you are ready to work in the PivotTable view, make sure the **Field List** button in the **Show/Hide** group on the **Design** tab under the **PivotTable Tools** contextual tab is highlighted. If not, click it to activate the dialog box.

Quickest Click: To add or move a field to and within the **PivotTable** view, grab the field name and drag it into the area on the **Object** pane where you want the field to go. The cursor will change **P** to show that you are moving a field and a mini-map of the table area will highlight the area of the **PivotTable** your field will drop into. Make sure you grab the field's name and not one of the field values.

 STOP

31

Add Calculated and Total Fields to PivotTable View

Difficulty: ●●●○

PROBLEM You have PivotTables that you are happy with, as they show you how well your sales team is performing in a given date range and what products they are selling. You would like, however, to use this information to tell you how many different kinds of products each sales member is selling and the average shipping costs of the items they are selling.

SOLUTION Use Total fields and Calculated detail fields. A calculated detail field uses an expression based on other detail fields. Total fields tally the values in the detail field.

See Also: Create a Calculation in a Query Field

Step-by-Step

Create a Total Field

1. Open the query that contains the **PivotTable** you want to work with and switch to **PivotTable View** from the **Views** group on the **Home** tab.

2. Select the field name of the values you want to total **A**, then make sure the **Show Details** button **B** in the **Show/Hide** group on the **Design** tab is highlighted. Click to highlight if it is not.

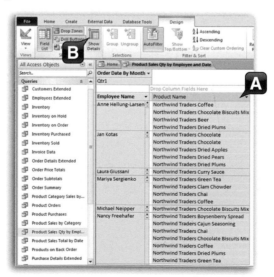

4. Click **AutoCalc** in the **Tools** group, then click the type of total you want to add:

- **Sum**: Totals the values in the field. Use with **Number**, **Decimal**, and **Currency** data types.

- **Count**: Counts the number of instances of a value. Use with all data types except complex repeating scalar data.

- **Minimum**: Calculates the smallest numeric value, the earliest date, or the first alphabetical value for text values. Use with **Number**, **Decimal**, **Currency**, and **Date/Time** data types.

- **Maximum**: Calculates the largest numeric value, the latest date, or the last alphabetical value for text values. Use with **Number**, **Decimal**, **Currency**, and **Date/Time** data types.

- **Average**: Averages the values by applying the formula "sum divided by count." The field must contain numeric, currency, or date/time data. The function ignores null values.

- **Standard Deviation**: Measures how widely values are dispersed from an average value (a mean). Use with **Number**, **Decimal**, and **Currency** data types.

- **Variance**: Measures the statistical variance of all values in the field. Can only use this function on numeric and currency data.

The **Total** field will appear in the **PivotTable Field List** dialog box  and a **Total** and **Grand Total** line will be added to the details area 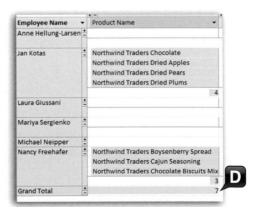.

Step-by-Step

Create a Calculated Detail Field

1. Open the query that contains the **PivotTable** you want to work with and switch to **PivotTable View** from the **Views** group on the **Home** tab.

2. Click **Formulas**  in the **Tools** group on the **Design** tab to open the dropdown menu, then click **Create Calculated Detail Field** to open the **Properties** dialog box.

3. Type a name for your calculated field in the **Name** text box **G**.

4. In the large text box, type the calculation you want to perform **H**. Select any fields you wish to use in the calculation by choosing it from the dropdown list **I** and then clicking **Insert Reference To** **J**.

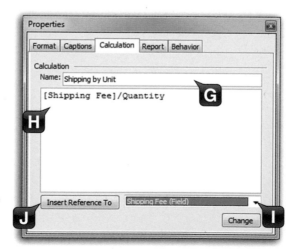

5. Click **Change**. Access adds the calculated field to the **PivotTable Field List** **K**.

6. Close the **Properties** dialog box. Add your calculated field to the **PivotTable** **L** as described in *Create a PivotTable View*.

32 | Create a PivotChart View

Difficulty: ●●●○

PROBLEM You have a query that shows you how many items each of your sales team has sold, the prices and shipping fees for each item, etc. You would like a way to quickly see how your sales members compare in number of units sold. You think a visual representation of the data would be the best way to understand and show the information.

SOLUTION Create a PivotChart View. A PivotChart is like a PivotTable in that you can manipulate different variations of your data to offer different interpretations using the same query.

The layout of a PivotChart is similar to a PivotTable, except that PivotCharts show data totals or summaries rather than data details. PivotCharts also show series and category areas where a series is a group of related data points represented by a particular color, and a category is a datapoint from each series represented by a label on the category axis.

See Also: Create Charts and Graphs

Step-by-Step

---

1. Open the query you want to make a **PivotChart** view from in the **Object Window**.

2. Create a **PivotTable** view that reflects the analysis you want. *See: Create a PivotTable View for a Query*

3. Click the **View** button in the **Views** group on the **Home** tab. Click **PivotChart View** **A**. A blank **PivotChart** **B** will open in the **Object Window** and the **Chart Field List** dialog box **C** will open.

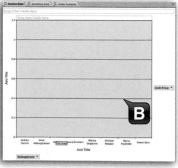

4. In the **Chart Field** List dialog box, click on the field you want to add to the chart, then select the area where you want the field to go **D** from the dropdown list at the bottom of the dialog box.

5. Click **Add to E**. ✳

6. Repeat the steps until you have added all the fields you want and your chart shows your information the way you want it. ⚠

7. To change the chart style, click the **Change Chart Type** button **F** in the **Type** group on the **Design** tab under the **PivotChart Tools** contextual tab to open the **Properties** dialog box. Select the new chart type from the left column **G**, then click on the chart style you want in the right column **H**. Your chart will reflect your choices in the object window **I**.

8. To delete a field from the **PivotChart**, click on its label in the chart and then press **Delete** on your keyboard. ✳

9. Click **Save** on the **File** tab or hit **CTRL+S** to save your **PivotChart** view for the query.

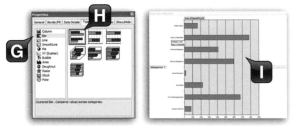

 Caution: Layout changes that you make in the **PivotTable** view will be reflected in the **PivotChart** view and vice versa. Be aware that modifying one can affect the other, with sometimes surprising consequences.

 Quickest Click: To add or move a field to and within the **PivotChart** view, grab the field name and drag it into the area on the **Object** window where you want the field to go. To remove a field from the **PivotChart**, grab the field's name and drag it away from the chart.

STOP

33 | Rename a Query Field

Difficulty: ●○○○

PROBLEM In your customer database, the field containing each customer's unique identifier is simply called "ID." Your customer data is accessed by several departments, including marketing, customer service, and sales. The problem is that each of those departments also has products and items with their own "IDs" (product IDs, catalog IDs, agent IDs, etc.).

SOLUTION Rename the field. You can rename any field in a query. A renamed field pulls the correct corresponding data from the database. Use this to clearly distinguish data and clarify terminology that is confusing or unfamiliar to other users of the database. To eliminate the confusion, you could change the field name display to "Customer Number."

Step-by-Step

1. Open the query you want to change in the object window.

2. If not already, switch your view into **Design** by clicking the **Design View** menu option **A** in the **View** dropdown menu in the **Views** group. 🔥

3. Click the field name you are editing **B**. In this example, the field name **ID** will be changed to display **Supplier Number**, instead of **ID**.

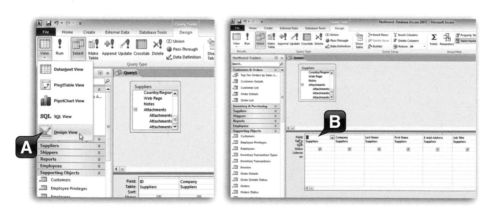

4. Place your cursor to the left of the first letter of the current field name.

5. Type the new field name (the one you want to display), followed by a colon. The result is structured: **Displayname: currentfieldname**. In this example, that is **Supplier Number: ID** 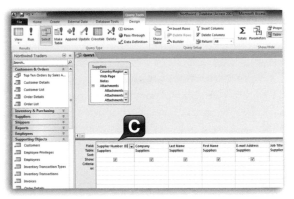.

6. Click the **View** button on the **Home** tab **D** to switch to **DataSheet** view.

7. Verify your new field name **E** appears as you intended.

 Hot Tip: In many cases, functions accessed from the **Ribbon** can also be found in right-click menus. For example, right-clicking a query's name shows you many of the same options available from the **View** dropdown button, including the **Design View** selection **F**.

34 Rename a Report Field

Difficulty: ●○○○

PROBLEM There is a Phone List report for all the participants in a charity event. There are two entries for phone number listed—home number and mobile number. However, when the phone numbers were entered, the number listed under "Home Number" is actually each participant's primary contact number. Looking at the report, there is no way to know this. Your colleague has asked for a copy of the report so that he may contact the participants.

SOLUTION Edit or Rename the field. Sometimes a field name in a report no longer makes sense or is not applicable to the viewers. Editing or renaming a field in a report is useful if you need to present existing report information more clearly.

Step-by-Step

1. Open the report that you want to edit **A**.

2. Click on the **View** dropdown in the **Views** group on the **Home** tab.

3. Select **Design View** **B**.

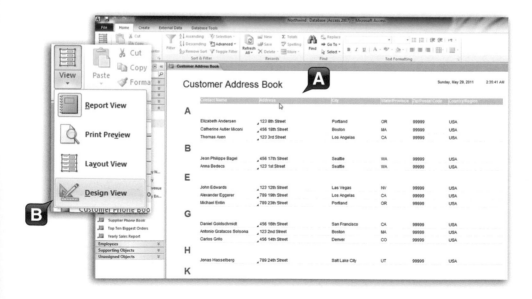

4. In the **Design View** of your report, select and highlight the text field you want to edit **C**.

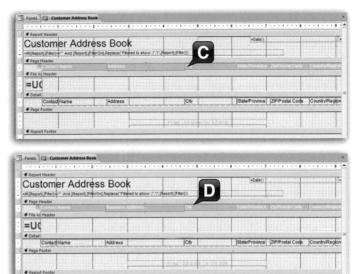

5. Type in the new value over the current selected text **D**.

6. Click **Save** on the **File** tab or type **CTRL+S** to save your report.

7. Click on the **View** button in the **Views** group on the **Home** tab.

8. Select **Report View E**.

9. Verify the edited field **F** and how it displays in the report.

35

Use the Group, Sort, and Total Pane to Organize Reports

Difficulty: ●●○○

PROBLEM You have created a report from your table of invoices that shows you the products you sold and how many were sold in each invoice. You would like to organize the information in a way that groups not only the products together, but also sorts by volume sold and groups dates into useful date ranges. In other words, you need to create a more complicated report with multiple levels of group and sort options.

SOLUTION Use the Group, Sort, and Total pane. Working in the Group, Sort, and Total pane gives you the greatest control over adding or modifying groupings, sort ordering and total options. Unlike just using the right-click option, you can create up to 10 group and sort levels in a report.

Step-by-Step

1. Open the report you want to modify in the object window.

2. If you are not already in **Layout** view, click the **Layout View** menu option **A** in the **View** dropdown menu in the **Views** group.

3. Click the **Design** tab under the **Report Layout Tools** contextual tab, then click the **Group & Sort** button **B** in the **Grouping & Totals** group to open the **Group, Sort, and Total pane C** below the object window.

4. To add a new sorting or grouping level, click the **Add a group D** or **Add a sort E** button. A new group or sort level will be created **F**.

5. Choose the field you want to group or sort from the **select field** dropdown menu **G** to add the group or sort level to the report. The changes will appear immediately in the object window.

6. To delete a group or sort level, select the row you want to remove, then press **Delete** on your keyboard or click the **Delete** button **H** to the right of the row.

7. Grouping and Sorting priority is determined by the level of the group or sort within the pane. The highest (or first) group will affect all the data, the next level will affect the data within the first group, and so on. In our example, the report groups invoices by Product, then groups by Order Date and then sorts by quantity. This will show us the number of units sold, from highest invoice to lowest, per product (rather than highest to lowest overall), per quarter.

   To change the priority level of a group or sort, select the row you want to move, then press the **Up** or **Down** arrows **I** to the right of the row until it is at the level you want.

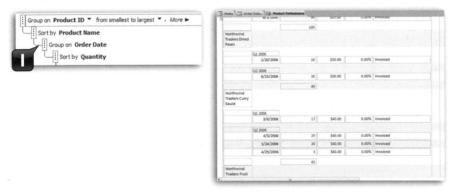

8. Click **Save** on the **File** tab or hit **CTRL+S** to save your report.

36 Edit Grouping, Sorting, and Total Options in Reports

Difficulty: ●●○○

PROBLEM You run a charity organization, and you want to create a report that shows a list of donors who were sent letters to renew their support and that shows how much they contributed over the past several years. You want to group the donation information by dates, but the default grouping of "by quarter" does not fit your needs. You also would like to show the largest and smallest amount each donor has given in those timeframes.

SOLUTION Customize your grouping, sorting, and total options in the Group, Sort, and Total pane. Each group and sort level has a number of options you can set to generate the report you need your data to show. In the example above, you can change the Group Interval option to group by year instead of quarter, and you can add Total rows that will show Maximum and Minimum total amounts instead of SUM totals.

See Also: Use the Group, Sort, and Total Pane to Organize Reports; Aggregate Query Data

Step-by-Step

1. Open the report you want to modify in the **Object** window.

2. If needed, switch your view to **Layout** view and open the **Group, Sort, and Total** pane.

3. Click on the sort or group level that you want to edit, then click the **More** button **A** to view all the options available for that level.

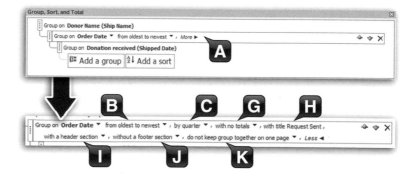

4. Click on the dropdown arrow of the option you want to adjust and change your settings:

- **Sort Order** **B**: Change the sort order options.

    Smallest to Largest or Largest to Smallest: applies to numeric values

    Oldest to Newest or Newest to Oldest: applies to date values

    With A on Top or With Z on Top: applies to text values

- **Group interval** **C**: Specify how records are grouped.

- By entire value, by first character, by first two characters or create your own custom grouping interval for text values **D**.

- By entire value, by day, week, month, quarter, or year; or create a custom grouping interval for dates **E**.

- By entire value; by 5s, 10s, 100s, or 1000s; or create custom grouping for numeric data **F**.

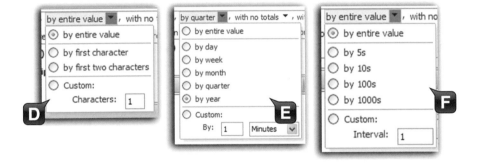

- **Totals** **G**: You can add totals to more than one field, and you can add more than one total to the same field. Set your preferences in the Totals dropdown menu:

    - **Total On** dropdown: Choose the field you want to create a total row for.

    - **Type** dropdown: Choose the type of calculation you want to perform.

    - **Show Grand Total**: Click the checkbox to add a grand total to the bottom of the report.

- **Show group subtotal as % of Grand Total:** Add a calculated field to the group footer that displays the group total as a percentage of the grand total.
- **Show in group header/group footer:** Click these to choose where you want the total displayed.

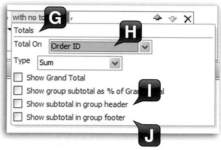

- **Title 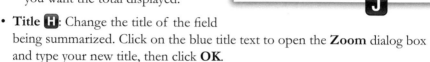**: Change the title of the field being summarized. Click on the blue title text to open the **Zoom** dialog box and type your new title, then click **OK**.

- **With/without a header section** : Add or remove the header section at the beginning of each group.

- **With/without a footer section** : Add or remove the footer section at the end of each group.

- **Keep group together** : Specify how the groups will look when printed.

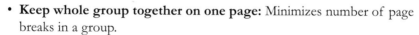

  - **Do not keep group together on one page:** Groups may be broken up by page breaks. Use to save paper or if you do not mind groups being split between pages.

  - **Keep whole group together on one page:** Minimizes number of page breaks in a group.

  - **Keep header and first record together on one page:** Ensures that group header will not print by itself at the bottom of a page before a page break.

5. Click **Save** on the **File** tab or hit **CTRL+S** to save your report.

Bright Idea: If you want your report to only show totals instead of groups of individual reports, click the **Hide Details** button  in the **Grouping & Totals** group on the **Design** tab for a much less cluttered report that focuses on the bottom line.

Hot Tip: You can also sort and group by expressions in your report to give you even more options for presenting your data. Click the **Add a Group** or **Add a Sort** button in the **Group, Sort, and Total** pane to add a new level. Click on the dropdown of available fields and select **Expression M** to open the **Expression Builder** dialog box. Enter the expression you want, then click **OK**.

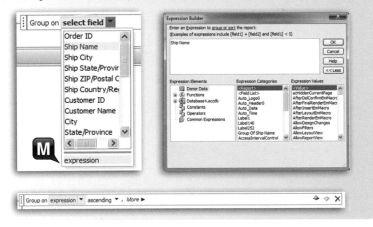

37 | Change Tab Order in a Form

Difficulty: ●○○○

PROBLEM Your coworker has collected registration forms for an upcoming charity walk. You need to enter all the data from the paper registration form into the database. In order to enter the information as quickly as possible, you would like to enter the items in the order they are listed, rather than look around the screen and bounce back and forth on your paper.

SOLUTION To create a more efficient form for the user, specify a custom tab order on the form. This means that when a user presses the Tab or Enter button on the keyboard, the cursor moves to the next field according to the order you have specified.

Step-by-Step

1. Open the form you want to change in the object window.

2. If you are not already in **Design** view, click the **Design** view menu option in the **View** dropdown menu in the **Views** group.

3. Click the **Design** tab **A**.

4. Click the **Tab Order** button **B** in the **Tools** group to open the **Tab Order** dialog box.

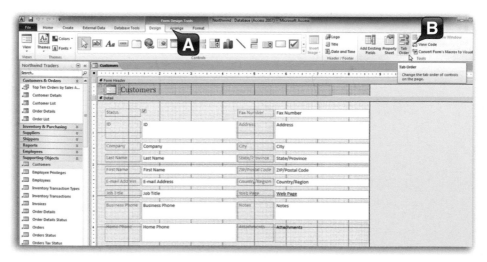

5. Click the part of the form you want to customize in the **Section** box 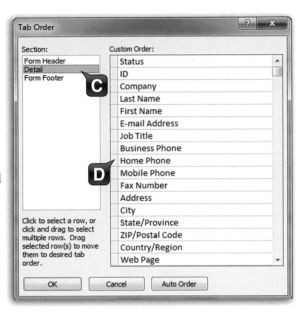 to open the tab field options in the **Custom Order** box.

6. To change the tab order, click inside the little box to the left of a row. **D** This highlights the row. Click and drag the row (your cursor must stay in the little box at the left of the row) to where you want the field.

7. Click the **OK** button.

 Hot Tip: Use the **Auto Order** button to change the tab order to how the fields are laid out on the screen. Access will put the fields in order based on their layout position on the form (i.e., top to bottom or left to right).

 Quickest Click: Remember—changing the order of the fields in this dialog box only changes the tab order; it does not change the order in which the fields are laid out on the screen. To change the field layout, edit the form to move the arrangement of your fields.

STOP

38 | Create and Use List Boxes

Difficulty: ●●○○

PROBLEM Your new customers have been invited to participate in a new program for free for the next six months. They have to choose a level of service from five different choices. As they return their program agreements, their information is added into the database. You want a way to easily record which service they have chosen without typing the choice over and over.

SOLUTION Use a list box. When you create a form, use the list box to display a list of data values. To simplify the data entry and avoid errors in typing incorrect information, display these five entries in a list box so the users can select the option in that field.

Step-by-Step

1. Open the form you want to change in the object window.

2. If you are not already in **Design** view, click the **Design View** menu option in the **View** dropdown menu in the **Views** group.

3. In the **Controls** group on the **Design** tab, click the **More** button to make sure the **Use Control Wizards** menu option **A** is highlighted. If it is not, click it to activate control wizards.

4. Click the **List Box** tool in the **Controls** group on the **Design** tab **B**.

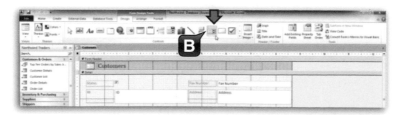

5. Click inside your form to create the default size list box or click and drag to create the size of your choice. The **List Box Wizard** automatically opens.

6. To pull the field data from another table or query, click the **I want the list box column to look up the values in a table or query** radio button **C**.

7. Click the **Next** button.

8. Select the table or query where you want to search for the selected values **D**. Refine the objects list by clicking on the **Tables** or **Queries** radio button; see all available objects by clicking the **Both** radio button.

9. Click the **Next** button.

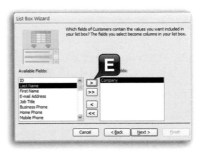

10. Select the field(s) from which you want to pull the values in the **Available Fields** box, and add them to the **Selected Fields** box using the **Add** button **E**.

11. Click the **Next** button.

12. To sort the values in the field by **Ascending** or **Descending** order click the dropdown arrow **F** to select a Field name.

13. Click the button marked **Ascending** to reveal **Ascending** order, or click it again to toggle to **Descending** **G**. Repeat the sort selection for each field you selected in the previous window.

14. Click the **Finish** button.

STOP

39

Create an Input Mask for Easier Data Entry

Difficulty: ●●●○

PROBLEM You want to make sure phone numbers are entered into your form in a standard 10-digit format with parentheses, such as (555) 555-1212.

SOLUTION Use an input mask. Input masks give users a guide to follow when entering data. An input mask can reduce errors and prevent incorrect data from being entered into fields. Input masks are useful when there is a standard format of the data, such as zip code information, password formats, Social Security Numbers, etc.

Step-by-Step

1. Open the form you want to work with in the object window.

2. If you are not already in **Design** view, click the **Design** view menu option **A** in the **View** dropdown menu in the **Views** group.

3. Click the field for which you want to create an input mask **B**.

4. Click in the **Input Mask** field in the **General** tab under **Field Properties** window **C**.

5. Click the **Build** button **D** to launch the **Input Mask Wizard.**

   Note: If Access prompts you to save the table first, click Yes.

6. Select the format (Phone Number, Social Security Number, Zip Code, etc.) that you wish to use for your **Input Mask E.**

7. Click the **Try It** textbox to test what this mask looks like.

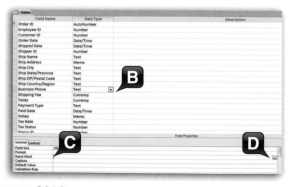

8. Click the **Next** button.

9. Choose a placeholder character to fill the spaces until an appropriate value is entered **F**.

10. Click on the **Try It** textbox to see what these placeholder characters will look like.

11. Click the **Next** button.

12. Select whether you want the data stored with or without symbols by selecting the appropriate radio button. It is a matter of usage as to whether presenting the symbols or not will make the data easier to analyze at first glance, such as (123) 555-1212 versus 1235551212. If the data can be used later in this format (as a plain number), you would want to eliminate the additional characters.

13. Click the **Finish** button.

14. Return to **Datasheet** view. Note that data in the field has changed to match your **Input Mask** parameters **G**.

Hot Tip: You can specify certain characters (such as # or *) to replace the text for the password entry on the screen, so the actual password is not visible as it is typed. If you work in an open workspace and sensitive information is entered into the database, use the **Password** input mask to limit the possibility of someone looking over a shoulder to obtain someone's password.

Create a User Interface (UI) Macro

Difficulty: ●●●○

PROBLEM You run a specific set of reports every morning that outline the overnight shipping activities for your small business. Instead of pulling these reports one by one and running each, you want to run them all with a single action.

SOLUTION Use a macro. A macro automates tasks and adds functionality to your database objects. Essentially, it is a shortcut for a frequently-run task. The macro can run the reports and e-mail them to your department heads on a daily basis, or it can simply open and/or print the reports.

>
> **What Microsoft Calls It:** Create a standalone macro

 Step-by-Step

1. Click on the **Create** tab **A**.

2. Click on the **Macro** button **B** in the **Macros & Code** group to launch the **Macro Builder.**

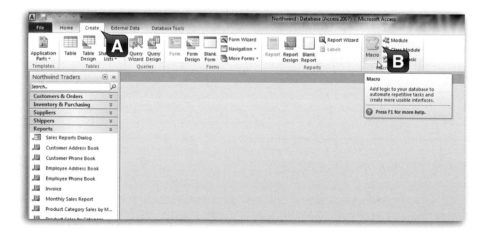

3. Select an action you want to run from the **Add New Action** dropdown list **C** and select the action you want to run. You can also browse or search for an action in the **Action Catalog** pane **D** where actions are grouped by category. Expand the categories to view the actions. When you find the one you want, drag them into the **Macro** lane. ⚡💡

There are approximately 70 different actions to choose from. The most commonly used actions include:

- **OpenReport**: this action opens the report you specify.
- **OpenTable**: this action opens the table you specify.
- **OpenQuery**: this action opens the query you specify.
- **OpenForm**: this action opens the form you specify.
- **FindRecord**: this action locates a specific record you specify.
- **OutputTo**: this action will output your directed action to a specified place. 💧

4. Fill in any arguments and preferences you need in the macro action to perform the task the way you want it to. For example, in the **OpenReport** macro action, you will need to specify the name of the report that the macro will open from the **Report Name** dropdown **E** and what view you want the report to display in when the macro has run from the **View** dropdown **F**.

5. If you want to add conditions or filters, enter those arguments in the corresponding text boxes or click the **Builder** button **G** to launch the **Expression Builder** dialog box.

6. Repeat steps 3-5 until your macro contains the complete sequence of events that you need.

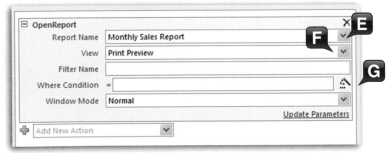

CONTINUE ▶

Create a User Interface (UI) Macro **113**

7. To change the order of the actions in your macro, click on the action in the **Macro pane** and drag it to the place you want it, or click the **Move Up** or **Move Down** buttons **H** on the right side of the action box. To delete an action, click the **Delete** button **I**.

8. Click the **Save** button or type **CTRL+S** to open the **Save As** dialog box. Type a name for your macro in the text box, then click **OK**.

9. To run your macro, double-click the macro in the **Navigation Pane** **J**.

Quickest Click: To add an action that opens a specific database object, drag the table, query, form, or report from the Navigation Page into the macro pane. Access will automatically add an action that opens the object. If you drag a saved macro into the macro pane, Access will automatically add an action that runs the macro.

Hot Tip: Access only lists those actions that will work in a non-trusted database. To see all the available actions, click the **Show All Actions** button in the **Show/Hide** group on the **Design** tab.

Bright Idea: Use embedded macros. An embedded macro is one that is embedded in an event property of an object and does not appear in the **Navigation Pane**, but rather is run from events such as **On Load** or **On Click.** When your stand-alone macro calls upon an object with an embedded macro, the embedded macro will run as specified, saving you from having to create more complicated stand-alone steps.

41 | Create a Data Macro

Difficulty: ●●●○

PROBLEM You want your sales team to stay on top of their accounts. To do so, you encourage each team member to contact their client when an order has been delivered and closed. You would like a way to notify each sales person when their account has closed an order.

SOLUTION Create a Data Macro that sends an e-mail each time a record is updated to "closed."

Data macros are a new feature of Access 2010 that let you add logic to events such as adding, updating, or deleting data. They are accessed from the **Tables** tab while viewing a table in Datasheet view. They do not appear under **Macros** in the **Navigation Pane**.

See Also: Create a User Interface Macro

 What Microsoft Calls It: Create an event-driven data macro

Step-by-Step

1. Double-click the table you want to add the data macro to open it in the object window.

2. Click the **Table** tab **A** under the **Table Tools** contextual tab.

3. Click the event that you want to trigger the macro **B**:
   Before Change
   Before Delete
   After Insert
   After Update
   After Delete

   The **Macro Builder** tab will open.

4. Add the macro actions you want your macro to execute *See Create a User Interface (UI) macro.*

5. Click the **Save** button or type **CTRL+S** to save the macro.

6. Data macros do not appear in the **Navigation Pane**. To find and edit your macro, open the table that contains the data macro you want to edit, then click on the **Table** tab. The events that have a macro associated with them will remain highlighted 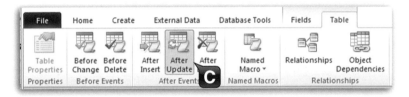.

 Hot Tip: You can also create a standalone data macro that remains associated with a specific table, but must be called by name rather than being triggered by an event. These are called named data macros and can be called from other macros with the **RunDataMacro** action. Named data macros can also use parameters that allow you to pass values in the macro for use in conditional statements or calculations.

Named data macros are managed on the **Table** tab from the **Named Macro** dropdown menu  and are created in the same way as event-driven data macros and standard macros.

STOP

42 | Create a New Table from a Query

Difficulty: ●●○○

PROBLEM You want to capture all sales data from the current quarter as it looks today and archive it. Since the data may change over time, re-running the query at a later date could produce different results.

SOLUTION Use a **Make Table Query**. A **Make Table Query** is useful when you need to make a new table that contains a copy of the data to export or to serve as a backup. The new table contains some or all of the fields and records from an existing table or combines the fields from two or more tables—similar to the results of a select query. A **Make Table Query** can also be used to share query results from one query within your current database with another database. Using a **Make Table Query** allows you to save the data from your query results into a table for future use.

Step-by-Step

1. In your selected database, open the query you want to use in **Design View** Ⓐ.

2. Click the **Make Table** button Ⓑ in the **Query Type** group of the **Design** tab.

3. In the **Table Name** textbox in the **MakeTable** dialog box, type the name of the new table you are creating Ⓒ.

4. If you are saving this table into another database, select the **Another Database** radio button. Otherwise, the system defaults to **Current Database**.

5. Click the **OK** button.

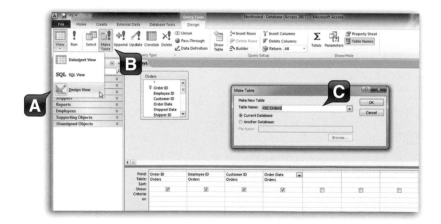

6. Click the **Run** button in the **Results** group of the **Design** tab **D**.

7. Click **Yes** **E** to create the new table that contains your selected records.

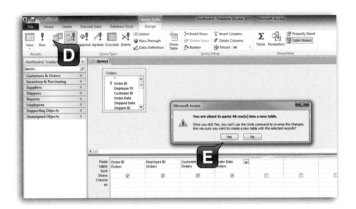

8. If you created your new table in the current database, the table name appears in your table list **F**.

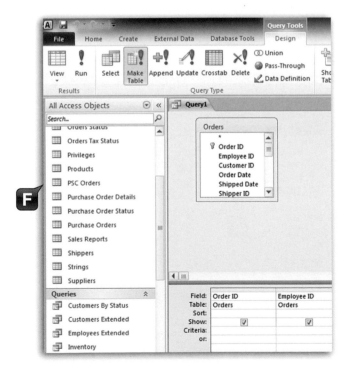

STOP

43 | Use a Query to Append Table Data

Difficulty: ●●●●

PROBLEM You work in the Finance Department in your organization. You have acquired a database from Human Resources. The database contains the names, starting salaries, current salaries, and other information for all employees. You already have a database with similar records. Rather than enter the additional information manually, you want to copy the records from the new database into your current one.

SOLUTION Use an append query to add new records to an existing table using data from other sources. 🔥

See Also: Preview Query Results

📚 Step-by-Step

1. Open the query with the records that you want to add to another table.

2. Click the **View** dropdown in the **Views** group of the **Home** tab and select **Design View** Ⓐ.

3. Click the **Design** tab Ⓑ.

4. In the **Query Type** group, click on the **Append** button Ⓒ.

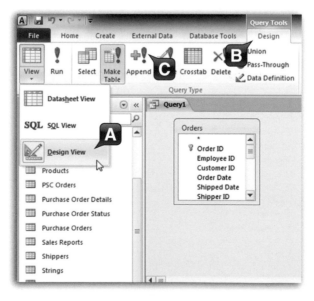

5. Select the database to which you want to append the data. If you select **Another Database**, browse to find the location and select it.

6. In the **Table Name** textbox, click the dropdown to view the table names available in your selected database **D** and select a table.

7. Click the **OK** button.

8. In your design grid, an additional row has been added called **Append To** **E**. If the field names in this row match the names of the fields you are appending, Access fills in the row with the names of the fields in the table to which you are appending. You will need to assign any that are missing using the dropdown box. ⚠

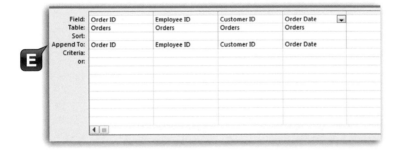

9. Click the **Run** button in the **Results** group of the **Design** tab **F**.

10. Click **Yes** to update the table that contains your selected records **G**.

11. Click the **Save** button to save this query for future use or close without saving if you will not use the query again.

12. Always check your results.

Caution: In the table where records are being added, do not append any data in an **AutoNumber** field, as Access automatically produces new numbers in the **AutoNumber** field for new records.

 Hot Tip: If you are only appending a few records, it may be easier and quicker to simply copy and paste the records from one table to another.

 Caution: Carefully check the **Append To** row on the design grid and make changes if necessary. The **Field** and **Table** rows show where the field comes from, and the **Append To** row shows where the data will be appended. If any fields don't have field names in the **Append To** row, display the dropdown list in the **Append** row and select the name of the field you want to append to. In addition, make sure that no field appears more than once in your **Append To** row.

Bright Idea: Use **Datasheet View** to see the results before you append them.

44 | Preview Query Results

Difficulty: ●○○○

PROBLEM You want to test a delete query before actually deleting any data.

SOLUTION View the query, rather than run it. In action queries, such as **Append, Make Table** and **Delete**, you can choose to view a query or run one. When viewing an action query in Datasheet view, you will see the results, but not execute the actions. This is useful when testing the results of your query to validate your actions. Running the query executes the action and deletes the data. ⚠

Step-by-Step

1. Open an action query in **Design View**.

2. Click on the **Design** tab.

3. In the **Results** group, select **Datasheet View A** to see the results or **Run** to execute the query.

4. After you review the results, select **Run B** to execute the action.

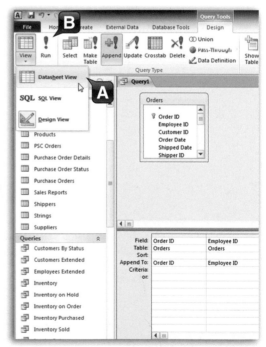

Caution: Once you execute (or run) a query, the results cannot be undone without recreating the query, which can be very time consuming. It is best to view your query before running it and always back up your database in case you need to retrieve the changed data.

45 Require a Password for a Database

Difficulty: ●●○○

PROBLEM You maintain a database that contains sensitive information protected by privacy rules. You want to make sure only authorized users are able to access this information.

SOLUTION Start by requiring a password for entry into your database. Requiring a password is also helpful for internal use, so only appropriate people can view, change, or update data and objects you are protecting. With enhanced privacy rules and thieves who make their living by stealing and selling information, it's more important than ever to protect data.

> **What Microsoft Calls It:** Encrypting the Database

Step-by-Step

1. Close any open databases and make sure that no other users have the database open.

2. Click the **File** tab **A** to open in the **Backstage** view.

3. Select **Open** **B**.

4. Select the database you want to open **C**.

5. Click the dropdown at the right edge of the **Open** button **D**.

6. Click **Open Exclusive** **E**.

7. Click the **File** tab to return to the **Backstage** view. Click the **Info** tab **F**.

8. Click the **Encrypt with Password** button **G** on the info pane to launch the **Set Database Password** dialog box.

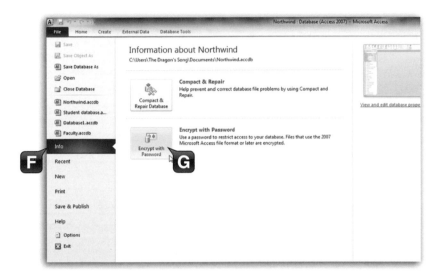

9. Type your password in the **Password** text box **H**.

10. Retype your password in the **Verify** textbox.

11. Click the **OK** button to activate the password protection.

 Hot Tip: Make a backup copy of your database and keep it in a secure place so if the password is lost or forgotten, you have access to a backup copy.

46 Create a Navigation Form to Simplify Database Use

Difficulty: ●●●○

PROBLEM Due to a new company initiative, you have thousands of new records to add into the database. You also have to run hundreds of new reports. You hire temporary help for the next two weeks to get this project completed on time. The staff is not experienced with Access.

SOLUTION Create a Navigation Form. Navigation forms are menus to help users find actions they need to take. If users enter data into multiple forms regularly, a navigation form provides a direct link to the actions that the users need to perform. You can create a form that takes your users directly to the forms they need to fill out or the reports they need to run, but without the ability to change or delete other objects. This allows them to get to their work quickly and easily while avoiding errors.

Step-by-Step

1. Open the database you want the form to access, then click the **Navigation** button **A** in the **Forms** group on the **Create** tab.

2. Select the style of form you want from the dropdown menu **B**. The new, blank form will appear in the object window in **Layout** view **C**.

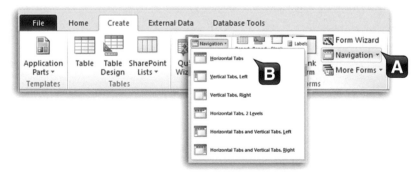

3. Make sure the Navigation pane is displayed. If it is not, hit F11 or click the double arrows **D** to the left of the object window to open it. Make sure the form is in **Layout** view **E**.

4. To add a form or report to the **Navigation Form**, drag the one you want into the **Add New** tab. Access will create a new navigation tab and display it in the object window **F**.

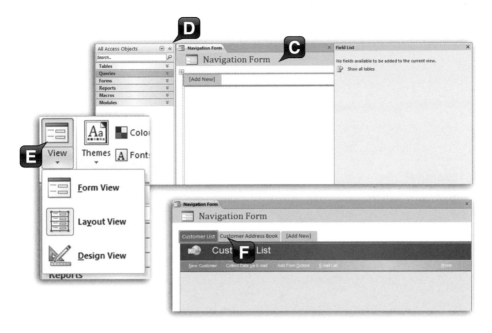

5. To edit the title of your **Navigation Form**, click in the form header to select it. Click again to edit the text to your preferred title **G**.

6. Press **Enter**.

7. If you want to change the look of a navigation tab or button, select the button you want to change, then use the tools in the **Control Formatting** group **H** on the **Format** tab to create your custom design **I**. 💡

8. Click the **Save** button or type **CTRL+S** to save your form. Type a name for your form in the **Save As** dialog box, then hit **OK**.

Create a Navigation Form to Simplify Database Use **129**

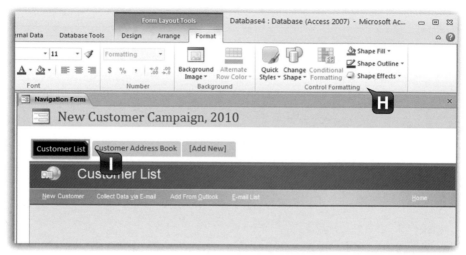

9. To set your navigation form as the default each time the database is opened, click the **File** tab, then click **Options**  to open the **Access Options** dialog box.

10. Click the **Current Database** tab **K**.

11. Under the **Application Options** heading, select your form from the **Display Form** list **L**.

12. Click **OK**. The navigation form you created will open automatically each time you open the database in Access. You will have to close and re-open the database for the default settings to take effect.

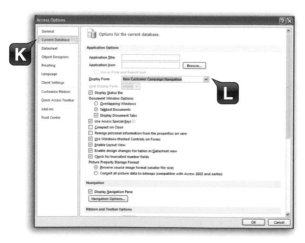

Bright Idea: You can apply a theme to your database. If you are creating a navigation form for general use, you can create a polished look that reflects your company colors and incorporates your company's logo in the reports and forms.

To apply a theme, choose from your theme options in the **Themes** group  on the **Design** tab. Choose colors from the **Colors** gallery, choose text treatment in the **Fonts** gallery, or pick a complete theme from the **Themes** gallery. Access will preview each theme choice when you hover over it.

47 | Create Rules to Control Data Entry

Difficulty: ● ● ● ●

PROBLEM Students in the regional high school's junior and senior classes are collecting money for the city's community center. A local car dealer donates a new car to be raffled to one student who collects $500.00 or more in donations for the cause. You have been asked to track those students who collect at least $500.00 or more. Someone else collects and maintains the data on money raised. You want to ensure the information is entered accurately.

SOLUTION Create a validation rule. Validation rules control what a user enters into a table field or form textbox. Create a validation rule to limit what data users can type into the database. To ensure there are only amounts over that $ limit, you can easily create a validation rule specifying that only a value greater than or equal to $500.00 may be entered into the field.

See Also: Appendix B—Validation Rules and Operations

 **What Microsoft Calls It:** Validation Rules

Step-by-Step

1. Open the table in which you want to create a validation rule in **Design View** 🅐.

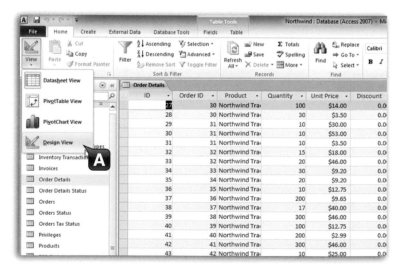

2. Click on the field where you want the data **Validation Rule** and change the **Data Type** if appropriate 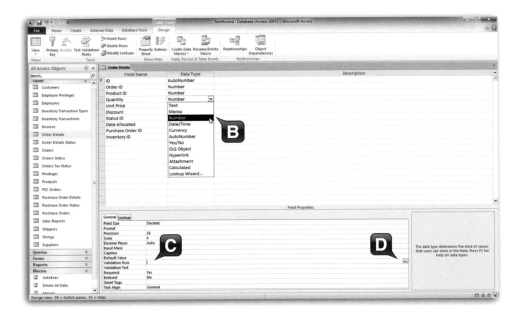.

3. Place your cursor in the **Validation Rule** textbox **C**.

4. Click the **Build** button **D** to open the **Expression Builder** dialog box.

CONTINUE

5. Create the validation rule. In this example, **>=10** is entered **E**, which specifies that values only greater than or equal to 10 are allowed. ⚡

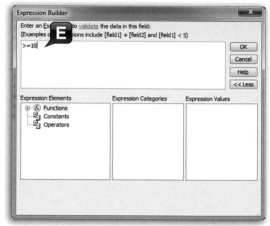

6. Click the **OK** button.

7. Place your cursor in the **Validation Text** textbox **F**. This is where you specify what text appears if entered values do not meet validation rules. In this example, "Value must be at lease 10" is entered.

8. Click the **Save** button on the **File** tab or type **CTRL+S** to save the table.

9. To test your validation rule, select the **Datasheet View** in the **Views** group on the **Home** tab.

10. To test the validation, type an "illegal" value into the table. The error message you created in Step 7 appears **G**.

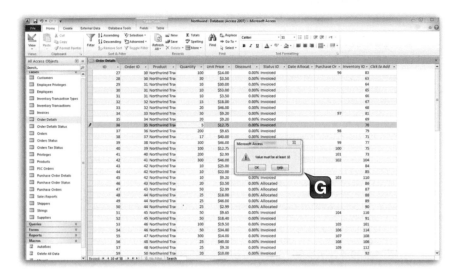

11. Click the **OK** button and retype a valid value, or leave the entry blank.

Quickest Click: Type your rule directly into the **Validation Rule** textbox if you are familiar with the operators. You do not have to open the **Expression Builder** to create your rule.

STOP

48 | Find and Replace Data

Difficulty: ●○○○

PROBLEM Although you can use a query to find data, sometimes you want to quickly find a few entries, such as specific employees or certain dollar amounts, or you may want to quickly change data to something else.

SOLUTION Use the **Find** and **Replace** commands. The **Find** feature allows you to quickly search tables, queries, and forms for specified text. Use the **Replace** command to quickly replace data with something else. The **Find** command in Access 2010 is similar to the same command in other Microsoft Office programs. However, it contains some additional features. For example, you can choose to match part or all of the data in a field.

Step-by-Step

1. Select the column header for the field you want to search or click in any cell in the field you want to search.

2. Click the **Find** button **A** in the **Find** group on the **Home** tab to launch the **Find and Replace** dialog box.

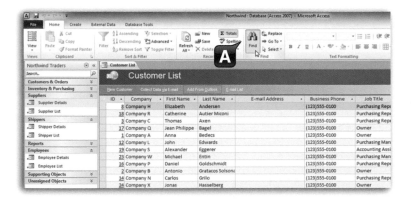

3. Type the text or value you want to find in the **Find What** textbox **B**.

4. If you are replacing the data with something else, click on the **Replace** tab **C**, and enter the replacement text value in the **Replace With** textbox **D**.

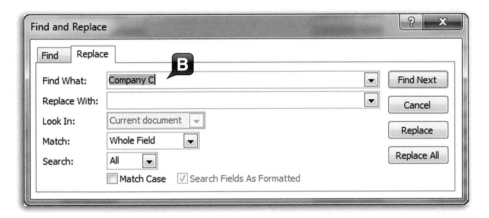

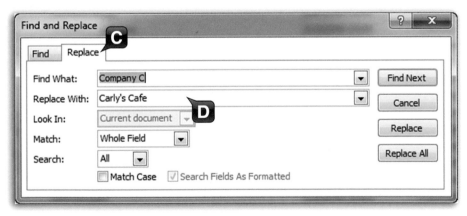

The following are the dialog box options and descriptions for the **Find and Replace** feature:

- **Find What** 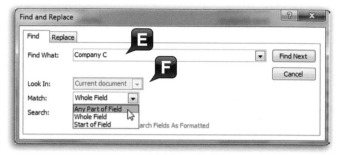: Type the value you are trying to find.

- **Look In** : Instruct Access to look for your data. This can be the field that the cursor is in or the whole table.

- **Match** : Choose how the search results match the **Find What** text. This option defaults to **Whole Field**. You can choose from:

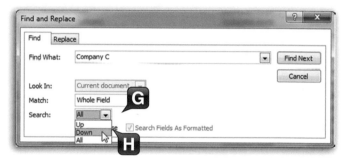

- **Any part of field**: usually finds the most instances. For example, if you search for the word "Car," you will find all values that have the value "car" anywhere in a field. This type of search would find "**Car**rie," "**Car**los," and "Ri**car**do," for example.

- **Whole Field**: finds only cells that match the whole field only. For example, if you are searching for "Antonio" and you put in "Ant" and search **Whole Field**, it will not work. In a **Whole Field** search, you must type in the whole value of your search item, in this case, "Antonio."

- **Start of Field**: finds cells that begin with your entered value. For example, if you type in "Ed," you will find "Edwards," "Edmonds," and "Eddick," but not "Redmond."

- **Search H:** Tells Access what direction you want it to search on your page. This depends upon where your mouse pointer is when you begin the search. This is useful when you have a large amount of data, and you have an idea of where the field you are searching for might be. If you know it is somewhere near the top of your datasheet, you might start at the top and move downward until you find it. If you are unsure, it is standard to search **All**.

  - **Up:** Access searches upwards from the current active cell. The search will not include anything below the active cell.

  - **Down:** Access searches downwards from your active cell. The search does not include anything above your active cell.

  - **All:** Access searches the whole datasheet, starting with the active cell.

 Caution: The default for the **Match** option is **Whole Field**. When searching text, people often enter part of a name because this type of search works in other Microsoft applications. Since it works differently in Access, it's important to specify the correct **Match** option.

 Quickest Click: Press **CTRL + F** on your keyboard to **Find** and **CTRL + H** to **Replace**.

49 | Export Data to Excel

Difficulty: ●●○○

PROBLEM You have information from a database that you need other users to analyze and manipulate, but they prefer to work in Excel.

SOLUTION Access 2010 allows users to export data out of Access and into Excel. Exporting data is a useful technique if you need to copy data from Access to Excel frequently. When data is exported, Access creates a copy of the selected data or object and stores the copy in an Excel worksheet. If you move data on a regular basis, automating this process will save time and effort.

Step-by-Step

Preparing to export

1. Open the database and select the object that contains the information you want to export. You can export a table, query, report, or form **A**.

    Note: Tables must be opened in **Datasheet View**. *To change the view of your object, click on the* **View** *button dropdown in the* **Home** *tab and select the applicable view* **B**.

    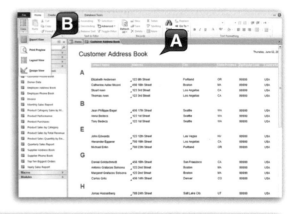

2. On the **External Data** tab **C**, in the **Export** group, click the **Excel** button **D** to open the Export Excel Spreadsheet dialog box.

3. Review the recommended file name and file location for the Excel workbook . Access automatically uses the name of the source object. If you want to change the file name, type in the new file name in this textbox.

4. In the **File Format** box **F**, select the file format that you want to use. If you are working with older versions of Excel, you may want to save the file down to an older version.

5. Next, specify export options. There are three options to review and select **G**:

- If you are exporting a table or query, and you want to export the data with the formatting parameters, select the checkbox for **Export data with formatting and layout**. If you are exporting a form or report, this option is always selected but unavailable and grayed out.

- To view the destination Excel workbook after the export operation is complete, select the checkbox to **Open the destination file after the export operation is complete**.

- If you have selected only certain records in your objects to export, select the checkbox to **Export only the selected records**.

6. Click **OK**.

7. If you selected the checkbox to open the destination Excel workbook after the export operation is complete, your Excel file opens up. Review your data for accuracy **H**.

8. Access will provide you with a
message displaying a "successful
operation." Choose whether you
want to save these export steps.
This allows you to repeat this
operation in the future with a
click. To save this export, click the
checkbox to **Save export steps** .

9. Click **Close**.

10. If you chose to save your export
steps, some additional fields
open up to complete. You may
enter a customized file name
and a description of the export
operation , though the Outlook
task option is a seldom-used
feature.

Hot Tip: Access allows you to create an **Outlook Task** that reminds you when it is time to run this operation. This is particularly helpful if you regularly repeat this saved operation (i.e., daily, weekly, or monthly). The **Outlook Task** will include a **Run Export** button that runs the operation in Access. To create the **Outlook Task**:

1. Select the check box 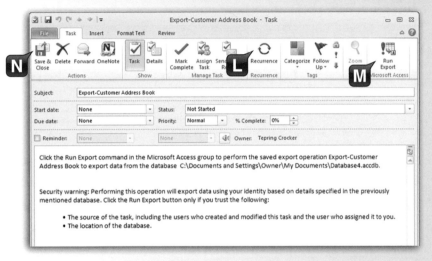 and click **Save Export**.
2. The **Outlook Task** will open. In this window, you can specify when or how often you want to complete this task by designating a recurring date/time to run task. Notice the **Run Export** button on the **Home** tab. When you have specified the task options, save and close the task by clicking the **Save and Close** button on the **Home** tab.

Option: You can only export one database object at a time. However, you can merge the data into multiple worksheets in Excel after you complete the individual export operations.

Caution: If the export operation fails because of an error, Access displays a message that describes the cause of the error.

STOP

50 | Prepare Excel Data for Use in Access

Difficulty: ●●○○

PROBLEM The Accounting department sends you a data dump of expense reports from their proprietary system, formatted for use in Excel, and you wish to import it into Access.

SOLUTION Excel and Access are compatible, but not interchangeable. Therefore, you need to properly prepare data before moving it from Excel into Access. Use this process when you have data created in an Excel worksheet, but you need that data to be entered and utilized within your Access database. When you prepare the worksheet to move the data into Access, you are cleaning up the extra formatting, functionality, and data that you do not need.

Step-by-Step

---

1. Open the worksheet you want to export in Excel.

2. Adjust column header titles so they contain no spaces or punctuation. Use underscores to replace spaces, but remove all other punctuation marks **A**.

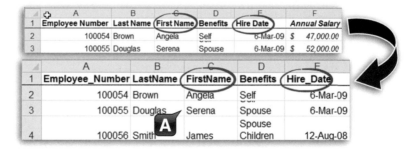

3. If the database contains the same or similar information, make sure:

    • Column headers match the corresponding headers from the database.

    • The same number of columns exists in the database and the spreadsheet information. ⚠

4. Format your worksheet as a table.

    • Select the data you want to define as a table **B**, including column headers.

- Click the **Table**
  button **C** in the
  Tables group of
  the **Insert** tab to
  launch the **Create
  Table** dialog box.

- Check the **My
  table has headers**
  checkbox **D**.

- Click the **OK**
  button.

5. Delete or remove
   blank columns, rows,
   and cells within
   the data. Eliminate
   records with empty
   cells, or insert a
   placeholder value
   (such as a 0 or NULL).
   Blank columns and
   rows at the "ends"
   of the sheet will be
   ignored.

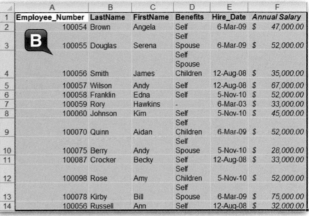

Caution: You need to keep the capabilities of each program in mind before you move data between the two, and you need to consider the nature of the data before you move it. For example, Access allows a number of links between various data tables. These links are not necessarily supported or easily demonstrable when you move the information to Excel. You may need to remove duplicate information or split your data into multiple sheets to create the most effective export.

STOP

51 Import Data from Excel

Difficulty: ●●●●

PROBLEM Your event manager keeps a log of people who sign up for your mailing list in Excel. She prefers to work in Excel and she brings you this data every few months. Sometimes the file contains hundreds of records that would take a long time to manually enter into Access.

SOLUTION Use the **Import Spreadsheet Wizard**. Import data from Excel when data that currently resides in an Excel worksheet is needed. This is useful when you have more than one piece of data in Excel that would take a long time and increase the possibility for error if entered manually. Access imports the data from an Excel spreadsheet into an Access table.

See also: Tip: Prepare Excel Data for Use in Access

 Step-by-Step

1. Click the **External Data** tab.

2. Click the **Excel** button in the **Import & Link** group **A** to open the **Get External Data – Excel Spreadsheet** dialog box.

3. In the **File Name** box **B**, enter the location of the Excel file from which you will import the data. Click the **Browse** button **C** to browse for the file.

4. Select the **Import the source data into a new table in the current database** **D** radio button or one of the other two choices **(Append a copy of the records to the table** and **Link to the data source by creating a linked table)** as needed.

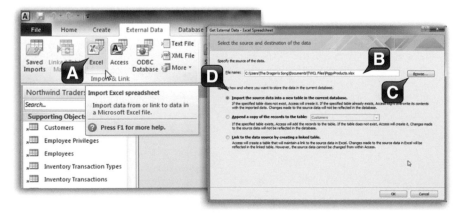

5. Click the **OK** button to open the **Import Spreadsheet Wizard**.

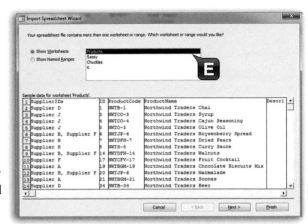

6. Select the individual worksheet from the Excel file you want to import **E**. You can only import one worksheet at a time. If your Excel file has only one worksheet, the wizard skips this step.

7. Click the **Next** button.

8. Select whether or not your Excel worksheet contains headings in the first row. If you select **First Row Contains Column Headings** **F**, Access imports the headings as field headings in the new table it creates.

9. Click the **Next** button.

10. The next step in the **Import Wizard** allows you to change a field name **G** and select a data type (i.e., text, currency, etc.) **H** for that field.

If a particular field contains a lot of data and will be searched frequently, select **Yes** from the **Indexed** dropdown list **I**. Indexing a column can make it faster to find data. If you check the **Do not import field (Skip)** **J**, the particular column you have selected will be removed from the table.

11. Click the **Next** button.

12. Select a **Primary Key** K. This is not required but strongly recommended.

13. Click the **Next** button.

14. In the **Import to Table** textbox L, enter a name for the new table.

15. Click the **Finish** button.

16. Select whether you want to save the import steps or not, then click the **Close** button.

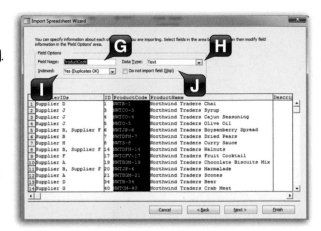

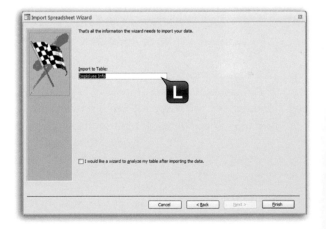

Bright Idea: If you regularly import the same worksheet to update your database, check the **Save import steps** checkbox and enter a name and description for the import **M**. To run your saved import, click the **Saved Imports** button **N** in the **Import & Link** group on the **External Data** tab to open the **Manage Data Tasks** dialog box. Choose from your saved imports and exports **O**.

52 | Collect Data through Outlook

Difficulty: ●●●●

Access works with Microsoft Outlook to create and send e-mail messages that include a form for data entry. Mail recipients can complete the forms and send them back to you. The responses are processed based on rules you establish, such as automatically adding responses to a table as soon as the messages reach your inbox.

For example, your Human Resources department annually updates emergency contact information for all employees. Using this function to collect data and automatically import it to the table saves hours of data entry and collection time. ⚠

Step-by-Step

1. Open the database in which you want your data stored.

2. Select the table in your navigation pane where you will store the data **A**. You can store data to two or more related tables by clicking on the query that binds these tables together.

3. Click on the **External Data** tab **B**.

4. Click the **Create E-mail** button **C** in the **Collect Data** group to open the **Collect data through e-mail messages** dialog box.

5. Click the **Next** button.

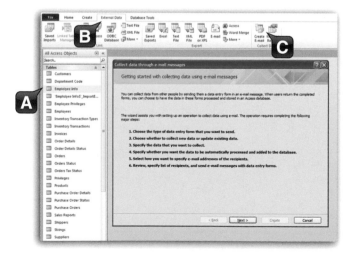

6. Select the data entry form (using HTML or InfoPath) by clicking the appropriate radio button **D**. The InfoPath option will be greyed out if you do not have InfoPath installed.

7. Click the **Next** button.

8. Select the appropriate radio button to specify whether you are **collecting new data** or **updating existing data**. 🌢

9. Click the **Next** button.

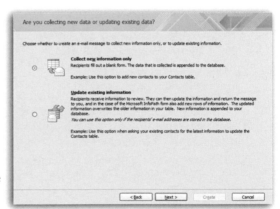

10. Select the fields to include in your form. Access automatically pulls the field names from the table or query you select. Click the **Add** button **E** to add one field at a time into the **Fields to include in e-mail message** box.

11. Highlight any of the fields to include in the e-mail and type a label for the field in the **Field Properties** box **F**.

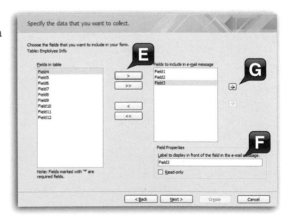

12. Click the up or dropdown to the right of the field boxes to move fields into different positions on the form, indicating the order in which you want them to appear **G**.

13. Click the **Next** button.

CONTINUE

14. Decide how you want to process your replies—manually or automatically—upon receipt of the reply e-mails.

- **Manually process replies:** Select each reply in Outlook, right-click, and choose **Export data to Microsoft Access.** This is also how you will manually process replies that fail to be automatically processed. To change the Outlook mailbox folder that your replies are stored in, click the **The replies will be stored in the following folder in your Microsoft Outlook mailbox:** Click link **H** to open the **Select Folder** dialog box. Browse to the folder you want, then click **OK**.

- **Automatically process replies and add data to table name:** Data is added to the table when Outlook and Access are open and responses are received. To have replies processed automatically, click the **Automatically process replies and add data to (tablename)** checkbox **I**. To customize the settings for how the replies will be processed, click the **Set properties to control the automatic processing of replies** link **J** to open the **Collecting Data Using E-mail Options** dialog box.

In this dialog box, you can specify import settings identifying whether you want to allow multiple replies from each recipient or allow multiple rows per reply. You can also set a limit to the number of replies you want processed and/or a date and time in which to stop running the process.

15. Click the **Next** button.

16. Select the appropriate radio button to specify how you want the recipients' e-mail addresses gathered. You can choose between:

- **Enter the e-mail addresses in Microsoft Office Outlook:** Create the list by typing in the addresses.

- **Use the e-mail addresses stored in a field in the database:** When e-mail addresses are stored in the database, you can pull them directly from the appropriate field. Specify whether the e-mail addresses are stored in the current table and select the field name—or direct Access to pull the e-mail addresses from another table, selecting the appropriate field name. This is the fastest way to create e-mail messages.

17. Click the **Next** button.

18. Customize the e-mail message by adding a **Subject** K and **Introduction** L. If you are using e-mail addresses stored in the a database field, you will also select which field you want the address inserted into M.

19. Click the **Next** button.

20. Click **Next** if you are using e-mail addresses from a database field or **Create** if you are going to enter addresses manually. ▲

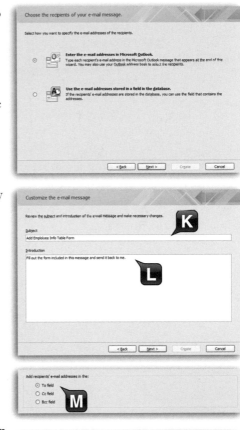

CONTINUE

- If you chose to enter the e-mail addresses manually, an Outlook email window will open. Add your addresses in the **To:** text box 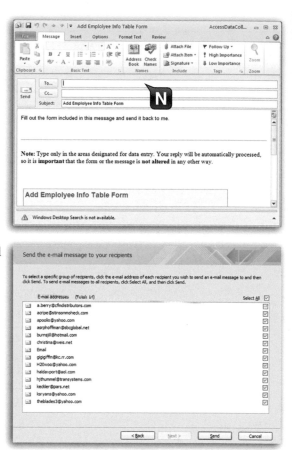, and then send your email as you normally would in Outlook.

- If you chose to use an e-mail address field from your database, the e-mail addresses will be listed in your main dialog box window. Deselect any e-mail addresses you do not want to send the message to and then click the **Send** button.

Caution: This feature can only be used if you have Office Access 2007 or later and Office Outlook 2007 or later. In addition, mail recipients must have an e-mail application that supports HTML format.

 Caution: The form used in this e-mail function is not an Access form. It is a form created using HTML and InfoPath. InfoPath is an optional feature. The InfoPath format cannot be used unless all users/recipients of the e-mail have InfoPath 2007 or later installed. The InfoPath form offers better data entry and editing, because it allows validation of the data by users before they send you the information. This prevents errors because users can view and edit their information before sending it.

 Caution: If you receive the error **The selected table or query does not have any fields that support collecting data using e-mai**l, your table may not contain any fields, or may have the following field types: AutoNumber, OLE Object, Attachment, or multi-valued lookup.

 Quickest Click: Right-click on the table or query and select **Collect and Update Data via E-mail.**

 Hot Tip: Collecting new data means that you are sending a blank form. This allows you to update existing information if the recipient has previously provided information for the database and his/her e-mail address is already in the database.

 Caution: Note whether you see any errors in the bottom textbox of this window. Access may provide an error that an e-mail address is incorrect or that you have an exclusive lock on the database (you must unlock the database to automatically process replies).

53 | Link to Excel with Copy and Paste

Difficulty: ●●●○

PROBLEM The Finance Director does a weekly revenue update using an Excel spreadsheet. She needs to pull updated information into her spreadsheet from the Sales Database in Access, and wants the information she needs to automatically update every time she opens her Excel spreadsheet.

SOLUTION Link Access and Excel.

When there is a need to link between Access and Excel, these links are established using OLE, or Object Linking and Embedding. This is a standard for sharing information among Windows programs. This enables you to create information in Access and display the information in Excel. The easiest way to establish a link between Access and Excel is to use Windows Copy and Paste functions.

Access pastes the information from the Clipboard into the Excel spreadsheet and establishes a link between this data and the original table or query you copied from. When you establish a link between Excel and Access, the information in Excel updates automatically. After you make changes in your Access database, changes automatically update when you open the Excel spreadsheet.

Step-by-Step

1. Highlight the table or query you want to link to Excel **A**.

    Note: You cannot establish an active link between Excel and only a portion of an Access table or query.

2. Click the **Copy** button **B** from the **Clipboard** group on the **Home** tab to copy the data to the **Clipboard**.

3. Open an Excel workbook and select the spreadsheet cell where you want the link to begin **C**.

Note: Data will fill cells to the right and down from your selected starting cell.

4. In the **Clipboard** group on the **Home** tab, click the dropdown on the **Paste** button and select the **Paste Special** option **D** to open the **Paste Special** dialog box.

5. Select **Paste Link E** at the left side of the dialog box. This forces a link between Excel and Access. ⚠

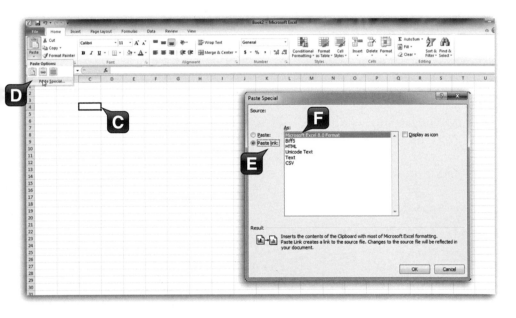

6. In the **As** list box **F**, select a data format option. Base the format you select on how you want your information to look once it is in Excel. The options include:

   - **Microsoft Excel 8.0 Format:** (Also known as Binary Interchange File Format BIFF8) Keeps Excel formatting and creates a link to the source file. This newest format protocol allows information to appear as close to the original as possible.

   - **Biff5:** Microsoft Excel Binary Interchange File Format, version 5.

   - **HTML:** Excel-pasted information in HTML format, which is the native format of the Web.

   - **Unicode Text:** The text of the original format is pasted using Unicode, or two-byte, characters. All other attributes (formats, appearance, etc.) are left up to Excel. Use this format when the original information contains foreign language symbols.

   - **Text:** Excel pastes the text of the original information. All other attributes (formats, appearance, etc.) are left up to Excel.

   - **CSV:** Excel interprets the incoming data as "comma separated values," meaning that it tries to break the fields based on locations of commas in the text. This is not a recommended format when pasting information from other Microsoft Office programs.

7. Click the **OK** button.

Caution: If you do not select **Paste Link** on the left side of the dialog box, it only pastes the data, not the link. Any changes you make to your data in Access do not carry over to your spreadsheet.

 Quickest Click: Press **CTRL+C** on your keyboard to copy or right-click on the table/query name and select **Copy**.

 Hot Tip: A faster way to paste in Excel is to click on the **Home** tab and press the dropdown on the **Paste** button and select **Paste Link.**

 Bright Idea: For all options except text, Access will transfer formatting details, such as font, row height, and column width. Access also transfers a header row. If you have an established link between Excel and Access with a header row, you cannot delete it.

54 Connect to an ODBC Database

Difficulty: ●●●●

PROBLEM The Project Management team collects monthly statistics on the status of all open projects and keeps the data in an Outlook folder. Finance wants an analysis of open project timeframes and percent-complete statistics compared with productivity and project status data from the Operations team, which is already in your database.

SOLUTION In Microsoft Access, you can query an external data source (such as an HTML page, or other database). You can link directly to .xml files over the Internet, Outlook folders, SharePoint, etc. The Project Management data can easily be imported into your database by querying Outlook and selecting the location of the data.

ODBC (Open Database Connectivity) links allow you to connect your Access database to external data sources. Use this to gain access to data that lives in another working data source, such as a database, spreadsheet, text file, etc.

For example, the Product database is too large to be directly imported into the Sales database. An ODBC link can be set up to access the required data through a link.

See Also: Query an External Data Source; Prepare Excel for Use in Access

---

 Step-by-Step

---

1. On the **External Data** tab, click the **ODBC Database** 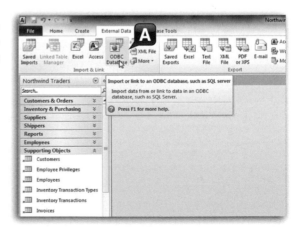 **A** button in the **Import & Link** group.

2. Select a radio button to choose how to store the data in your current database **B**.

    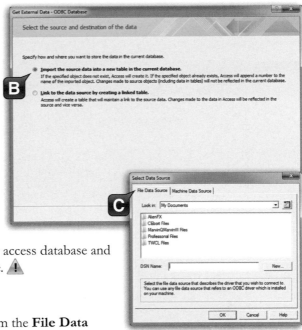

    - **Import the source data into a new table in the current database:** Import brings all the data from the external data source to your computer. Use this if the data does not change.

    - **Link:** Link maintains a live link between your access database and the external data source.

3. Click the **OK** button.

4. Select the data source from the **File Data Source** tab **C** or the **Machine Data Source** tab **D**.

    *Note: If you select **Machine Data Source**, this data is specific to your machine and cannot be shared. If you select **File Data Source**, you can select data from any files you have access to, which may be shared.*

5. Click the **OK** button.

Caution: If you have suitable permissions, you may manipulate data in the external data source, even if owned and operated by someone else. Check this before establishing a connection.

Hot Tip: You may be prompted for a username and password if you connect to an encrypted database. You may also need to specify which tables you want to connect with. Be sure you have the information before initiating the connection.

STOP

Explore Available Views and Screen Layouts

Every object in Access has different views, which are ways of looking at and working with the data contained in each object.

Object		View	Description
Table		Design View	Opens the table so you can add, delete, or edit fields.
		Datasheet View	Displays the table data as rows in an unformatted worksheet.
		PivotTable View	Displays a PivotTable creation interface.
		PivotChart View	Displays a PivotTable and PivotChart construction interface.
Query		Design View	Opens the query so you can add, delete, or edit fields, criteria, and any run actions.
		Datasheet View	Displays the query results as rows in an unformatted worksheet.
	SQL	SQL View	Displays the query's representation in the Structured Query Language (SQL).
		PivotTable View	Displays a PivotTable creation interface.
		PivotChart View	Displays a PivotTable and PivotChart creation interface.

Object		View	Description
Form		Design View	Opens the form so you can add, delete, or edit fields and controls.
		Form View	Displays the form data using your designed layout.
		Datasheet View	Displays the form data as rows in an unformatted worksheet.
		Layout View	Displays report so you can change its size. Also allows you to change the size and position of its sections, headers, and footers.
		PivotTable View	Displays a PivotTable creation interface.
		PivotChart View	Displays a PivotTable and PivotChart creation interface.
Report		Design View	Opens the report so you can add, delete, or edit fields and controls.
		Report View	Displays the table or query data with your designated formatting.
		Print Preview View	Displays the report as it will print.
		Layout View	Displays report so you can change its size. Also allows you to change the size and position of its sections, headers, and footers.

STOP

B | Validation Rules and Operations

Operator	What It Means	How to Use It
<	Less than	Looking for a value less than another. <10
<=	Less than or equal to	Looking for a value less than or equal to another. <=10
>	Greater than	Looking for a value greater than another. >10
>=	Greater than or equal to	Looking for a value greater than or equal to another. >=10
NOT	Looks for converse values. Use before any comparison operator except IS NOT NULL.	NOT > 10 (not greater than 10). This can also be written as <=10.
IN	Looks for values equal to existing members in a list. Comparison value must be a list, separated by commas, in parentheses.	IN ("Hawaii," "California," "Kentucky," "Massachusetts")
BETWEEN	Looks for a range of values. You must use two comparison values —low and high—and you must separate those values with an AND separator.	Between 500 and 1000. This can also be written >=500and<=1000.
LIKE	Matches pattern strings in Text and Memo fields.	LIKE "*ing" (see wildcard character listing on next page)
IS NOT NULL	Forces users to enter values into the field. This is the same as setting the Required field property to Yes. However, this enables you to enter custom Validation Text, as opposed to the system-provided error message.	IS NOT NULL
AND	Specifies that all the data that you enter must be true or fall within the limits you specify.	>=#01/01/2007# AND <=#12/31/2007#
OR	Specifies that one or more pieces of data can be true.	Red OR Blue

Wildcard	What It Means	How to Use It
?	Any single character	This symbol replaces any single character. For example, to specify a parameter for entering a US state abbreviation, enter ??. To search for a record for Mark vs Marc, enter Mar?.
#	Any single number	This symbol replaces any single number. To specify a parameter or search for a phone number, use this symbol. (###) ###-####. If you know the last four digits of a phone number are 1234, but want to search for the rest of the number, enter (###) ###-1234.
*	Zero or more characters	This symbol is useful when you search for part of a word. For example, to find all records with the customer's last name starting with "Mon" (such as Monroe, Montague, and Monard), type in Mon*.

STOP

C | Keyboard Shortcuts

Menu Shortcuts	
Show the shortcut menu (same as Right-click)	**SHIFT+F10**
Show the access keys (see "Magic Alt Key")	**ALT or F10**
Toggle the Navigation Pane	**F11**
Cycle between open windows	**CTRL+F6**
Restore the selected minimized window when all windows are minimized	**ENTER**
Turn on Resize mode for the active window when it is not maximized; press the arrow keys to resize the window	**CTRL+F8**
Display the control menu	**ALT+SPACEBAR**
Close the active window	**CTRL+W or CTRL+F4**
Switch between the Visual Basic Editor and the previous active window	**ALT+F11**

General Shortcuts	
Open a new database	**CTRL+N**
Open an existing database	**CTRL+O**
Exit Access 2010	**ALT+F4**
Print the current or selected object	**CTRL+P**
Open the Print dialog box from Print Preview	**P or CTRL+P**
Open the Page Setup dialog box from Print Preview	**S**
Cancel Print Preview or Layout Preview	**C or ESC**
Save a database object	**CTRL+S or SHIFT+F12**
Open the Save As dialog box	**F12**
Open the Find tab in the Find and Replace dialog box (Datasheet view and Form view only)	**CTRL+F**

Open the Replace tab in the Find and Replace dialog box (Datasheet view and Form view only)	**CTRL+H**
Find the next occurrence of the text specified in the Find and Replace dialog box when the dialog box is closed (Datasheet view and Form view only)	**SHIFT+F4**
Copy the selected control to the Clipboard	**CTRL+C**
Cut the selected control and copy it to the Clipboard	**CTRL+X**
Paste the contents of the Clipboard in the upper-left corner of the selected section	**CTRL+V**
Delete the selection or the character to the left of the insertion point	**BACKSPACE**
Delete the selection or the character to the right of the insertion point	**DELETE**
Delete all characters to the right of the insertion point	**CTRL+DELETE**
Undo typing	**CTRL+Z or ALT+BACKSPACE**
Undo changes in the current field or current record; if both have been changed, press ESC twice to undo changes, first in the current field and then in the current record	**ESC**
Select the next field	**TAB**
Switch between Edit mode (with insertion point displayed) and Navigation mode in a datasheet. When using a form or report, press ESC to leave Navigation mode.	**F2**
Switch between selecting the current record and the first field of the current record, in Navigation mode	**SHIFT+SPACEBAR**
Extend selection to the previous record, if the current record is selected	**SHIFT+UP ARROW**
Select all records	**CTRL+A or CTRL +SHIFT+SPACE**

Entering & Editing Data	
Move to the beginning of the entry	**HOME**
Move to the end of the entry	**END**
Move one character to the left or right	**LEFT ARROW or RIGHT ARROW**
Move one word to the left or right	**CTRL+LEFT ARROW or CTRL+RIGHT ARROW**
Select from the insertion point to the beginning of the text entry	**SHIFT+HOME**
Select from the insertion point to the end of the text entry	**SHIFT+END**
Change the selection by one character to the left	**SHIFT+LEFT ARROW**
Change the selection by one word to the right	**CTRL+SHIFT+RIGHT ARROW**
Move to the next field	**TAB or RIGHT ARROW**
Move to the last field in the current record, in Navigation mode	**END**
Move to the previous field	**SHIFT+TAB, or LEFT ARROW**
Move to the first field in the current record, in Navigation mode	**HOME**
Move to the current field in the next record	**DOWN ARROW**
Move to the current field in the last record, in Navigation mode	**CTRL+DOWN ARROW**
Move to the last field in the last record, in Navigation mode	**CTRL+END**
Move to the current field in the previous record	**UP ARROW**
Move to the current field in the first record, in Navigation mode	**CTRL+UP ARROW**
Move to the first field in the first record, in Navigation mode	**CTRL+HOME**
Insert the current date (in a Datasheet or Form)	**CTRL+SEMICOLON (;)**
Insert the current time (in a Datasheet or Form)	**CTRL+SHIFT+COLON (:)**

Insert the default value for a field (in a Datasheet or Form)	**CTRL+ALT+SPACEBAR**
Insert the value from the same field in the previous record (in a Datasheet or Form)	**CTRL+APOSTROPHE(')**
Add a new record (in a Datasheet or Form)	**CTRL+PLUS SIGN (+)**
In a datasheet, delete the current record	**CTRL+MINUS SIGN (-)**
Save changes to the current record	**SHIFT+ENTER**
Switch between the values in a check box or option button	**SPACEBAR**
Insert a new line (in a Datasheet or Form)	**CTRL+ENTER**

The "Magic" ALT Key

When you press the **ALT** key on your keyboard, letters appear on the ribbon 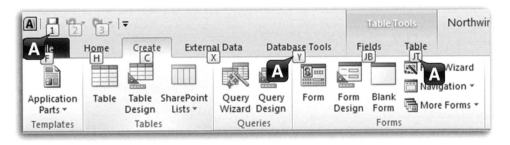. Typing a letter launches the corresponding function. Unlike other keyboard shortcuts, **ALT** shortcut keys are pressed sequentially, not held down at once. This can be much faster than using the mouse.

Index